MW01241788

ANNUAL SERMON STARTERS VOLUME 1

By Barry L. Davis

Copyright©2016 Barry L. Davis

GodSpeed Publishing

ISBN-13: 978-1530495634
ISBN-10: 1530495636

Looking for more Sermon Resources?

Visit Us at: <u>www.SermonSubscription.com</u>

Introduction

Dear Fellow Preacher,

For most of us, one of the most rewarding, yet difficult tasks, is preparing messages to preach and teach. We are honored by God to stand before our congregation each week, and we want to give them the very best, but with the press of the many demands of ministry, sometimes that is difficult to do.

And if you're like me, you prefer writing your own sermons because you have a special connection with your congregation that is hard to reach through a message someone else has written. In other words, no one knows your people like you do!

Our Annual Sermon Starters Series gives you a starting point – a sermon title, a deductive sermon outline; and a relevant introduction/illustration you can use however you like. Most of the sermon starters belong to a series. We have also included a number of Holiday Sermon Starters at the beginning of this Volume.

You are free to "fill-in-the-blanks" so to speak, and add your own meat and potatoes to the mix! We invite you to make these messages your own, because only you know the people God has called you to preach to.

And we are so honored that you've invested in this first volume of the Annual Sermon Starters Series – there will be more to come!

May God Bless You as You Share His Word!

In Christ,

Barry L. Davis

Barry L. Davis, D.Min., Ph.D.

Table of Contents

Mother's Day: "Leaving a Legacy"

Introduction:

[1]CITIZEN, a publication from FOCUS ON THE FAMILY, reported the online auction of a "mother's touch."

Dan Baber honored his mother by posting an auction on eBay titled, "Best Mother in the World." The winning bidder would receive an e-mail from his mom, Sue Hamilton, that Baber promised would "make you feel like you are the most special person on the Earth."

How did people respond to Baber's offer? "During the auction's seven-day run, 42,711 people—enough to fill most baseball stadiums—took a look. Ninety-two bid, pushing the price from a $1 opening to a $610 closing."

It's interesting how many are willing to pay for something most mothers give for free.

Moses' mother shared her touch with Moses throughout his life. You remember Moses? Moses is one of the most familiar names in the Bible. In fact, his name is referenced more than 800 times in Scripture. But here's a pop quiz for you: What was his mother's name? Most people would have a hard time answering that question. As a mother she left an incredible legacy, but like most Moms she doesn't get a lot of recognition or appreciation. Her name is only mentioned twice in Scripture – her name is *Jochebed.*

To a great extent a Mother's Legacy is defined by her children, and Moses wasn't

Jochebed's only child. Before Moses, there was Aaron—the older brother who ended up being Moses' right hand man when God delivered the Israelite slaves out of Egypt and who was the first High Priest. And before Aaron was Miriam—the woman who ended up

---

[1] *Focus on the Family: Citizen (July 2002), p. 12*

being one of the worship leaders for the Israelites after they crossed the Red Sea.

Miriam, Aaron, and Moses. That kind of legacy doesn't happen by accident. So let's look at the life of Jochebed and get a glimpse into the life of this mom who left behind an incredible legacy and see how our moms can do the same.

1. SHE WAS A POSITIVE ENCOURAGER

Exodus 2:2

Exodus 2:2 (Message Paraphrase)

2. SHE WAS AN INTENTIONAL DISCIPLER

Exodus 2:2-8

Deuteronomy 6:6-7

3. SHE WAS A FAITHFUL FOLLOWER

Hebrews 11:23

Father's Day: "God's Kind of Father"

Introduction:

Whatever happened to masculinity? Where can we go to find good role models for our sons? Not necessarily tough guys or muscle men – just men who know that they're men.

It seems that our society is trying to redefine the roles of men/women. In Chuck Swindoll's book *Growing Wise in Family Life*, he asks the following questions:

Remember when men were men? Remember when you could tell by looking? Remember when men knew who they were, liked how they were, and

didn't want to be anything but what they were? Remember when it was the men who boxed and wrestled and bragged about how much they could bench press? Remember when it was the women who wore the makeup, the earrings and the bikinis? Remember when it was the men who initiated the contact and took the lead in a relationship, made lifelong commitments, treated a woman like a lady, and modeled a masculinity that displayed security and stability?

Swindoll goes on to say, "We need fewer spineless wimps who've never disentangled themselves from mama's apron strings, and more clear-thinking, hard-working, straight-talking men who, while tender, thoughtful, and loving, don't feel the need to ask permission for taking charge. I'm convinced that most single ladies would love to have men like that to spend time with...and most wives long to have men like that to share life with. Children especially like having dads like that."

Did you catch that last line? "Children especially like having dads like that." I think Chuck Swindoll is on to something here: Our children are looking to us to be examples of real masculine men.

The children of our world are crying out for fathers that are actually wanting to fulfil the masculine role God has intended for them – that is they want fathers who will take on the spiritual leadership of their home; fathers who will be there when they need them; fathers who are willing to accept the responsibility that was given them when they became fathers.

Of all the fathers named in the Bible, Abraham stands out as the kind of father God wants every father to be. Concerning Abraham, God said:

"For I have chosen him, that he may command his children and his household after him to keep the way of the LORD by doing righteousness and justice, so that the LORD may bring to Abraham what he has promised him." – **Genesis 18:19 (ESV)**

Abraham was a man of great faith, obedience, generosity, and prayer. He is truly one of the most outstanding men in the Bible and is worthy of being imitated by all men, especially fathers. From Abraham we learn what God's Kind of Father is like.

1. HE IS A MAN WITH GOD'S CALL ON HIS LIFE

Ephesians 6:4

2. HE IS A MAN WITH GOD'S BLESSING IN HIS LIFE

3. HE IS A MAN WITH A GRACIOUS SPIRIT

Genesis 13

Genesis 21

4. HE IS A MAN OF GREAT PRAYER

Genesis 15

Genesis 17

5. HE IS A MAN OF GREAT FAITH

Hebrews 11:8-9

Hebrews 11:10-11

Hebrews 11:17

Genesis 15:6

Thanksgiving: "Abounding in Thanksgiving"

Introduction:

For most of us, there is one day out of the year when we take the time to celebrate all the wonderful things God has done for us and to give Him thanks. And the idea of setting apart a day to show gratitude to God is a great thing, but I'm thinking we need to take it well beyond that – God is expecting, and deserving, of much more than one day of thanksgiving.

What He desires from us is a life of thanksgiving, where every day is spent in celebration and gratitude to God. And while at first hearing, that might sound like a difficult thing to do, it really isn't as hard as we might think for those who are believers in Christ. Indeed, the Apostle Paul gave us instruction on how to do just that:

Therefore, as you received Christ Jesus the Lord, so walk in him, rooted and built up in him and established in the faith, just as you were taught, abounding in thanksgiving. – **Colossians 2:6-7 (ESV)**

In this short passage of scripture we are taught how we as Christians can live a life of thanksgiving if we're simply willing to do what God asks us to do. There are four statements that I am going to make based on this text that I am hoping you will adopt as your very own. Because if you do, not only will you live every day in gratitude for God, but you are also going to get blessed in the process as we shall see.

1. I'M OBLIGATED TO OBEDIENCE

...walk in Him.

> Matthew 28:20

> Matthew 11:29

2. I'M DEDICATED TO DEVELOPMENT

...rooted and built up in Him.

3. I'M CULTIVATING MY CONVICTIONS

...established in the faith, just as you were taught.

Matthew 19:14

4. I'M EXPRESSING MY PRAISE

...abounding in thanksgiving.

Easter: "Easter – Facts and Acts"

Introduction:

[2]Ken Davis tells about a woman who looked out of her window and saw her German shepherd shaking the life out of a neighbor's rabbit. Her family did not get along well with these neighbors, so this was going to be like a disaster.

She grabbed a broom, pummeled the dog until it dropped the now extremely dead rabbit out of its mouth. She panicked. She did not know what else to do. She grabbed the rabbit, took it inside, gave it a bath, blow dried it to its original fluffiness, combed it until that rabbit was looking good, snuck into the neighbor's yard, and propped the rabbit back up in its cage. An hour later she heard screams coming from next door. She asked her neighbor, "What's going on?" "Our rabbit! Our rabbit!" her neighbor cried. "He died two weeks ago. We buried him, and now he's back!"

What I have to talk to you about today is of utmost importance to the church…and not just this church, but to the church of Jesus Christ in all its various expressions. On this day, Easter Sunday, we commemorate the resurrection of Jesus Christ from the dead. Sometimes I think that we've gotten so used to saying it, that the actual reality of what we are talking about somehow gets lost in the process.

We are talking here about Jesus, after having been nailed to the Cross, and experiencing complete and total death, literally coming back to life again. We are talking here about a body that was as far removed from life as that body you saw at the last funeral you attended, having lungs refilled with oxygen, blood coursing through its veins again, and brain activity returning back to normal.

And if that wasn't enough, the body that literally rose from the dead was none other than the body of God in human flesh, who died three

---

[2] http://www.kendavis.com/video/the-rabbit-and-the-hound/

days previously for the sins of the entire world. If we can't get excited about that, somebody better check our pulse.

"Easter is the truth that turns a church from a museum into a ministry." – Warren Wiersbe

The most fundamental truth of the entire Bible is that Jesus rose from the dead. Without the resurrection, the rest of the Bible becomes pretty much meaningless. In fact, when we read about the history of the early church in the book of Acts, we discover that the resurrected Christ was the topic they were to proclaim throughout the world.

And we are witnesses of all that he did both in the country of the Jews and in Jerusalem. They put him to death by hanging him on a tree, but God raised him on the third day and made him to appear, not to all the people but to us who had been chosen by God as witnesses, who ate and drank with him after he rose from the dead. And he commanded us to preach to the people and to testify that he is the one appointed by God to be judge of the living and the dead. To him all the prophets bear witness that everyone who believes in him receives forgiveness of sins through his name." – **Acts 10:39-43 (ESV)**

What Peter proclaimed so many years ago, is the same thing we need to be proclaiming today – and that's what I want today. I've broken this message up into two parts – the first is *Facts – What You Need to Know*, and the second is *Acts – What You Need to Do*. If we can get a handle on these two things, this is going to be the best Easter ever.

FACTS – WHAT YOU NEED TO KNOW:

There are three specific things you need to know, whether you are already a Christian, or if you're thinking about becoming one.

1. JESUS DIED FOR YOU

1 Peter 2:24

2. JESUS ROSE FOR YOU

Luke 24:6-7

3. JESUS CARES FOR YOU

John 3:16-17

ACTS – WHAT YOU NEED TO DO:

1. DIE TO YOURSELF

Matthew 16:24

2. LIVE FOR JESUS

3. RISE WITH JESUS

John 11:25-26

1 Corinthians 15:20

Gifts of Christmas: "The Gift of Strength"

Introduction:

During this Christmas season we have the great privilege of spending some time together, discovering the gifts that God wants to give to each one of us. Today we want to find out about, and accept, the Gift of God's Strength.

I have no doubt that some of you sitting here are in great need of God's Strength right now. Some of you are dealing with grief, with uncertainty concerning the future, with serious health issues, with difficult relationships, with overwhelming temptation, with doubt, with depression, with success, etc.... and you're not sure how to overcome. And if this is not a time of weakness or vulnerability in your life, you will be tested at some point in the future, because it comes to all of us. The great news is that God wants to give you His gift of Strength so that you are no longer depending on your own power to see you through.

1. WHAT WE NEED TO KNOW ABOUT GOD'S STRENGTH

1) He is a Powerful God

2) He is an Empowering God

Psalm 29:4-11

2 Timothy 1:7

2. WHAT WE NEED TO DO TO RECEIVE GOD'S STRENGTH

Step 1: Affirm God's power and His presence

1 Chronicles 16:11-12

Joshua 1:9

Step 2: Admit your own weakness

2 Corinthians 12:9

Step 3: Align yourself with God's will

John 15:5

Step 4: Ask God for the power that you need

James 4:2b

Step 5: Act right now out of obedience to God

1 Peter 5:6-7

Gifts of Christmas: "The Gift of Joy"

Introduction:

[3]Once there was a little boy who was really mean. No matter what his parents tried, he continued to be self-centered and selfish. Christmas was coming soon, so the little boy, in his usual selfish way, made his "Dear Santa" letter – it was twelve pages of gadgets and toys.

When his parents saw the monstrous letter, they were outraged. The father picked up the little boy and carried him to the living room, setting him firmly on the floor right in front of the family's nativity scene. "I want you to sit right here and look at this scene until you remember what Christmas is all about. Then I want you to write a letter to Jesus."

So the little boy sits there a while and then returns to his bedroom. Finding paper and pencil, he begins to write: "Dear Jesus, if you will bring me all the presents I want, I'll be good for a whole year." Then he thinks for a moment and tears up the paper. He starts again: "Dear Jesus, if you'll bring me all the presents I want, I'll be good for a whole week," but once again he tears up the paper. The little boy quietly leaves his room and returns to the living room, looking intently at the nativity scene. He gently reaches down and picks up the figure of Mary. Returning to his room, he places the figure in a shoebox and sets the box in the back of his closet. Then he writes another letter: "Dear Jesus, if you ever want to see your mother again..."

Last week we talked about the gift of strength that God wants to give us this Christmas. Today we're going to learn about another gift that God wants to give – the Gift of Joy. One of the first things ever said about Jesus was that He was coming to bring joy. An angel appeared to some shepherd's in their fields and said:

---

[3] 1001 More Humorous Illustrations for Public Speaking, Zondervan Publishing.

"Fear not, for behold, I bring you good news of great joy that will be for all the people. For unto you is born this day in the city of David a Savior, who is Christ the Lord." – **Luke 2:10-11(ESV)**

This is what the nation of Israel had been waiting to hear! Their deliverer had come! The Messiah, the Chosen One, the bringer of deliverance was here. The news of the birth of Christ brought joy to the hearts of the people. It was not an insignificant kind of joy that expresses itself in a moment of laughter. It was the kind of joy that settles deep down in your gut – the kind of joy that remains even when there's nothing to laugh at, or nothing to celebrate. It is a deep-seated joy that cannot be taken from you no matter what circumstance you might find yourself in.

The angel said that this "good news of great joy" was "for all the people." Not only for the people of Israel, but for all people of all time who would willingly accept this good news into their hearts. In fact, Peter writes to those, like us, that have never seen Jesus face to face:

Though you have not seen him, you love him. Though you do not now see him, you believe in him and rejoice with joy that is inexpressible and filled with glory. – **1 Peter 1:8 (ESV)**

How can I accept this gift of joy that God wants to give to me? How can I continue to live with this level of joy and satisfaction throughout my life? I have put together four statements for us that, if lived out, will allow us to not only receive God's gift of joy, but will enable us to walk in joy throughout our lives. I am going to ask you to personalize these statements in your own life today.

1. I WILL ACCEPT GOD'S FREEDOM

Romans 8:1-2

Acts 16:34

Psalm 51:12

2. I WILL DWELL IN GOD'S PRESENCE

Psalm 16:11

Isaiah 56:7a

Jeremiah 15:16

3. I WILL OBEY GOD'S INSTRUCTION

John 15:9-11

4. I WILL EXPECT GOD'S FUTURE

1 John 2:17

1 Peter 1:4-5

Philippians 3:20-21

Gifts of Christmas: "The Gift of Christmas"

Introduction:

I'm sure you all remember that song, "The Twelve Days of Christmas"? It is kind of a fun song to sing, but have you ever really thought about the "gifts" the true love is giving on the different days?

A Partridge in a pear tree; 2 Turtle Doves; 3 French Hens; 4 Calling Birds; 5 Golden Rings; 6 Geese A-laying; 7 Swans A-swimming; 8 Maids A-milking; 9 Ladies Dancing; 10 Lords A-leaping; 11 Pipers Piping; 12 Drummers Drumming

These sound like some of the lamest gifts of all time! This is a "true love" giving us these presents? I can imagine opening up the box, "Wow, this is just what I was hoping for honey, a partridge in a pear tree! You're the greatest!"

I know that on Christmas morning some of you will open up some presents far more useful than any of these. But we've been discovering over the last couple weeks some gifts that God wants to give us that are more valuable than anything you are going to find under your tree.

We've learned that God wants to give us the Gifts of Strength and Joy. But today we want to learn about the Gift of Christmas itself. We're going to talk about the Relevance, the Reason, and the Result of this gift.

1. THE RELEVANCE: GOD CAME TO EARTH

Colossians 1:15-17

Philippians 2:7

2. THE REASON: GOD CAME FOR OUR BENEFIT

1) To Show Us What He Is Like

2) To Show Us How to Live

Matthew 16:25

3) To Show Us We Can Trust Him

4) To Show Us How to Be Forgiven

1 John 3:5

Philippians 2:6-8

1 John 4:9-10

3. THE RESULT: YOU CAN KNOW GOD IN RELATIONSHIP

Romans 5:10-11

Philippians 2:9-11

Gifts of Christmas: "The Gift of Hope"

Introduction:

Several years ago Dr. Harold Wolff conducted a study for Cornell University Medical School. A part of his study involved 25,000 U.S. soldiers who were POWs during WWII. Many prisoners died, and most became sick under the terrible conditions, inhumane treatment, and forced labor. But strangely enough, Dr. Wolff discovered a few who showed only slight physical change during their nightmarish months in prison.

What made the difference? Dr. Wolff discovered an above-average ability to hope in the men who survived and were healthy. They were looking to, and planning for the future they expected to have. Dr. Wolff concluded that when a person has hope, he is capable of incredible burdens and unbelievably cruel punishment. But when he has no hope, he simply can't survive.

We have to have a hope for tomorrow that gives us the courage and strength to go on today. We have to know a better day is ahead, or we'll give up. What oxygen is to the lungs; what blood is to the heart; what food is to the body; what water is to the tree; what gasoline is to the automobile; so is hope to the human heart – It's the ingredient that keeps us going.

During the month of December we've been talking about the Gifts that God wants to give to us – we've learned about the gifts of Strength, Joy, and the gift of Christmas. Today, I want to focus on the gift of hope that God wants to give us. The gift of hope is the gift of knowing that our future is in heaven with God. We're going to look at a number of verses in Revelation 21 and 22 that help us to better understand the hope that is ours in Jesus Christ. These chapters specifically describe the scene in heaven for those who have placed their trust in Jesus Christ.

1. WHERE DO I FIND HOPE?

Revelation 21:6

2. WHAT CAN I LOOK FORWARD TO?

GOD WILL TAKE AWAY...

Fear

Revelation 21:1

Sorrow

Revelation 21:4

Temple

Revelation 21:22

Evil

Revelation 21:23-25

GOD WILL GIVE...

Protection

Revelation 21:12a

Revelation 21:16-21

Participation

Revelation 22:3

Revelation 22:5

Provisions

Revelation 22:1-2

Perception

Revelation 22:4

Starting Over: "I'm Going to Set My Priorities"

Introduction:

[4]A minute is a funny amount of time. It's long enough to notice, but it's too short to do much of anything with. There are only about five hundred thousand of them in a year. But when you add all of humanity together, a lot starts to happen in that lowly minute. Consider what happens before the second hand of a clock completes one rotation:

- **25** Americans will get a passport, according to the U.S. Department of State.
- **58** airplanes will take off around the world, according to the International Air Traffic Association.
- **116** people will get married, according to data from the United Nations.
- **144** people will move to a new home, according to Gallup.
- **11,319** packages will be delivered by UPS.
- **243,000** photos will be uploaded to Facebook.
- **5,441,400** pounds of garbage will be created, according to the World Bank.
- **7,150,000,000** human hearts (according to the United States Census Bureau) will beat ... **500,500,000,000** times, according to the American Heart Association, as their bodies create ... **858,282,240,000,000,000** new red blood cells, according to the National Institutes of Health.

The question is, what are we doing with our minutes? How are we spending our time? When it comes to our day-to-day existence, we need to decide what our priorities will be in life – because every minute counts. In our new series beginning today, *Starting Over*, we want to wipe the slate clean and begin our lives all over again. And the first thing we have to do is set our priorities in life.

---

[4] ROBINSON MEYER, "WHAT HAPPENS IN ONE MINUTE AROUND THE WORLD?" *The Atlantic* (3-14-14)

Today we are going to look at the three main priorities each of us should have as Christians.

1. GOD IS MY FIRST PRIORITY

1) We Worship Him

Luke 4:8

2) We Obey Him

1 Peter 1:14-16

3) We Accept Our Status as His Children

John 1:12-13

2. MY FAMILY IS MY SECOND PRIORITY

1) To Provide a Christian Home

Joshua 24:15

2) To Live by God's Standard

Ephesians 5:21-26

Ephesians 6:1-3

3. MY CHURCH IS MY THIRD PRIORITY

Romans 12:4-5

1) To Find My Area of Service

2) To Depend on Others

Starting Over: "I'm Going to Follow Jesus"

Introduction:

[5]To illustrate Christ's call to discipleship, Pastor Tommy Hinson shared that on some evenings, he and his son, Riley, enjoy watching YouTube videos of Space Shuttle launches together.

Hinson said that there is a point at the end of the video where you hear the phrase "negative return."

According to NASA's official website, "negative return" occurs when the space shuttle "is flying too far downrange and too high to return to the launch site in the event of an engine failure." It also means that, for the astronaut, they are now to the point where they are assured of making it into orbit—which is the whole point of the shuttle launch.

Hinson comments:

Jesus is saying, only by crossing the point of "negative return," letting go of the option to turn back, can you actually do what you're meant to do. Whatever your landing site was—your identity, your sense of purpose—before you came to me, you need to leave all possibility of returning behind.

Some of you committed your lives to Jesus years ago, but for some reason you need to recommit and return to that decision you made long ago. For others, this might be the very day that you make that decision. As we continue in our series, *Starting Over*, you have those opportunities before you. But just to be clear, let's look today at exactly what you are committing to when you decide to follow Jesus.

1. I AM COMMITTING TO CHRIST'S LORDSHIP

---

[5] TOMMY HINSON, SERMON "HARD SAYINGS OF JESUS: HATE YOUR PARENTS," CHURCH OF THE ADVENT (9-8-14)

Matthew 7:22-27

2. I AM COMMITING TO CHRIST'S CHURCH

Ephesians 1:22-23

3. I AM COMMITTING TO CHRIST'S PEOPLE

Serve one another	Galatians	5:13
Accept one another	Romans	15:7
Forgive one another	Colossians	3:13
Greet one another	Romans	16:16
Bear one another's burdens	Galatians	6:2
Be devoted to one another	Romans	12:10
Honor one another	Romans	12:10
Teach one another	Romans	15:14
Submit to one another	Ephesians	5:21
Encourage one another	1 Thessalonians	5:11

4. I AM COMMITTING TO CHRIST'S PURPOSE

1) Serve

Matthew 20:28

2) Save

Luke 19:10

3) Share

John 10:10

Starting Over: "I'm Going to Discover My Purpose"

Introduction:

[6]Four psychologists did a study of notable quotations from famous people around the world about the meaning of life. The study analyzed the quotes of 195 men and women who lived within the past few hundred years. Here's a summary of the major themes and some of the people representing each theme:

1. *Life is primarily to be enjoyed and experienced. Enjoy the moment and the journey.*
   17 percent of the famous people in the study endorsed this theme (Ralph Waldo Emerson, Cary Grant, Janis Joplin, and Sinclair Lewis). Janis Joplin is best known for her lyric: "You got to get it while you can."

2. *We live to express compassion to others, to love, to serve.*
   13 percent endorsed this theme (Albert Einstein, Mohandas Gandhi, and the Dalai Lama). Albert Einstein stated: "Only a life lived for others is a life worthwhile."

3. *Life is unknowable, a mystery.*
   13 percent endorsed this theme (Albert Camus, Bob Dylan, and Stephen Hawking). Hawking wrote, "If we find an answer to that (why we and the universe exist), it would be the ultimate triumph of human reason—for then we would know the mind of God."

4. *Life has no meaning.*
   11 percent endorsed this theme (novelist Joseph Conrad, Sigmund Freud, Franz Kafka, Bertrand Russell, Jean Paul Sartre, and Clarence Darrow). Darrow compared life to a ship that is "tossed by every wave and by every wind; a ship

---

[6] RICHARD KINNIER, JERRY KERNES, NANCY TRIBBENSEE, CHRISTINA VAN PUYMBROECK; *The Journal of Humanistic Psychology* (WINTER 2003)

---

headed to no port and no harbor, with no rudder, no compass, no pilot, simply floating for a time, then lost in the waves."

5. *We are to worship God and prepare for the afterlife.*
   11 percent endorsed this theme (Desmond Tutu, Billy Graham, Martin Luther King Jr., and Mother Teresa). Desmond Tutu said, "[We should] give God glory by reflecting his beauty and his love. That is why we are here, and that is the purpose of our lives."

6. *Life is a struggle.*
   8 percent endorsed this theme (Charles Dickens, Benjamin Disraeli, and Jonathan Swift). Swift wrote that life is a "tragedy wherein we sit as spectators for awhile and then act our part in it."

7. *We are to create our own meaning of life.*
   5 percent endorsed this theme (Carl Sagan, Simone DeBeauvoir, and Carl Jung). Carl Sagan wrote: "We live in a vast and awesome universe in which, daily, suns are made and worlds destroyed, where humanity clings to an obscure clod of rock. The significance of our lives and our fragile realm derives from our own wisdom and courage. We are the custodians of life's meaning."

8. *Life is a joke.*
   4 percent endorsed this theme (Albert Camus, Charlie Chaplin, Lou Reed, and Oscar Wilde). Charlie Chaplin described life as "a tragedy when seen in close-up but a comedy in the long shot." The rock star Lou Reed said "Life is like Sanskrit read to a pony."

With only a couple of exceptions, this is a very sad list. For some people, life is pretty much meaningless, with no real purpose, or value at all. For others, purpose in life is what drives them, motivates them, and moves them forward.

Today, as we continue our series on *Starting Over*, I'd like to share with you the story of another man who had a lot to say about this subject many years before – a man we know as the Apostle Paul.

Paul made it very clear in his writings in the Bible that our main purpose as human beings was to live our lives, not for ourselves, but for the glory of God.

And the thing that I have discovered, as have many of you, is that when we seek first and foremost to bring glory to God, our lives are blessed as a result. There are five specific lessons about purpose in the text we'll look at today.

1. PURPOSE DEFINES WHO WE ARE

Philippians 1:12

2. PURPOSE DIRECTS OUR FUTURE PATH

Philippians 1:12

3. PURPOSE TESTIFIES TO OUR FAITH

Philippians 1:13

4. PURPOSE EQUIPS OTHERS FOR MINISTRY

Philippians 1:14-17

5. PURPOSE CAUSES US TO CELEBRATE

Philippians 1:18-19

Starting Over: "I'm Going to Focus on Relationships"

Introduction:

[7]In 2013, consumers paid $2.2 billion worldwide to find a mate and the overall market is expected to continue to grow at about 5 percent a year over the next five years. Dating through mobile is exploding and now accounts for roughly 27 percent of the dating site services, but it has remained a persistently weak spot for much of the industry. An article in The New York Times also noted the rise of niche dating sites, including **GlutenfreeSingles**.com, **TrekPassions**.com, **SeaCaptainDate**.com, **DateMyPet**.com and **TheAtlasphere**.com, for devotees of Ayn Rand's libertarian philosophy.

I have known some couples who have met, gotten married, and had a positive relationship after meeting on an online dating service. I've also met others who have had a very unpleasant experience.

But what does the growth of these, and other social networking type sites tell us? It tells us that people are hungering for viable relationships. Of course, relationships do not have to be romantic ones. Often we seek friendships, and the sharing of things we have in common with others.

At this church we value authentic, loving relationships where true Christian fellowship is practiced. And through that fellowship with each other, we are also fellowshipping with God.

> If we walk in the light, as he is in the light, we have fellowship with one another, and the blood of Jesus his Son cleanses us from all sin. – **1 John 1:7 (ESV)**

Do you see how the two are tied together? When we truly access God through fellowship, our fellowship with each other grows to a

---

[7] BY LESLIE KAUFMAN AND MIKE ISAAC, "IAC/INTERACTIVECORP MAKES MOVES IN ONLINE DATING," *The New York Times (9-15-14)*

whole new level. And it is through this type of fellowship with each other, that we are able to further access the God whom we worship. I am hoping today that some of you are ready to *Start Over* in this area of your life, as it is such an important element to your Christian growth.

Today I'd like us to consider two different texts in John's Gospel that help us to better understand what it means to truly be in relationships with others. And as we look at these texts, note that we are viewing fellowship as synonymous with love for each other, because that is the heart of fellowship.

1. RELATIONSHIPS COMMANDED

John 13:34-35

1) We are to love others as Jesus loves us (v. 34)

2) Our love for others indicates our love for God (v. 35)

2. RELATIONSHIPS TESTED

Test 1: Friends Do for each other

John 15:13

Test 2: Friends Share with each other

John 15:15

Test 3: Friends Love the same things

John 15:11-12

Test 4: Friends Please each other

John 15:14

3. RELATIONSHIPS PRACTICED

1) At Our Church God comes First

2) At Our Church People come before Programs

3) At Our Church Community is Central

John 17:20-23

Take Off Your Mask:
"Dealing with Conflict"

Introduction:

We are starting a new series today we are calling, "Take Off Your Mask." Our key verse is 2 Corinthians 4:2 from "The Message" paraphrase:

We refuse to wear masks and play games. We don't maneuver and manipulate behind the scenes. And we don't twist God's Word to suit ourselves. Rather, we keep everything we do and say out in the open, the whole truth on display, so that those who want to can see and judge for themselves in the presence of God. – **2 Corinthians 4:2 (MSG)**

The idea is that many people masquerade as something they really are not, or pretend things don't bother them that do, or act like they believe something they really do not, or twist things to fit someone else's perception. In other words, there are masks that all of us wear, and when we wear these masks we are not being honest with ourselves, with those around us, or with God.

One of the masks we wear is in the area of conflict.

[8]A Danish health survey asked almost 10,000 people between ages 36 and 52, "In your everyday life, do you experience conflicts with any of the following people—your partner, children, other family members, friends, or neighbors?" Eleven years later, 422 of them were no longer living. That's a typical number. What's compelling, the researchers noted, is that the people who answered "always" or "often" in any of these cases were two to three times more likely to be among the dead. (And the deaths were from standard causes: cancer, heart disease, alcohol-related liver disease, etc.—not murder.)

---

[8] JAMES HAMBLIN, "STRESSFUL RELATIONSHIPS VS. ISOLATION: THE BATTLE FOR OUR LIVES," *The Atlantic* (5-13-14)

The researchers concluded, "Stressful social relations are associated with increased mortality risk among middle-aged men and women." That's why they recommended that we develop what they called "skills in handling worries and demands from close social relations as well as conflict management."

But in case you think that all conflict is bad, people who said they "never" experience conflict from social relationships had a slightly higher mortality rate than those who "seldom" do. In other words, perhaps a little conflict is good for your health.

Even in laughter the heart may ache, and the end of joy may be grief.
– Proverbs 14:13 (ESV)

Each of us experiences conflict, some to a greater degree than others. The issue for us today isn't whether we have conflict or not, but how we should deal with it in the best way. When conflict comes, it is not uncommon to do one of the following things:

> 1) **Dominate it** – no discussion, no conversation, no trying to work it out.
>
> 2) **Ignore it** – pretend there is no conflict and let life go on as usual.
>
> 3) **Whine about it** – complain and complain, but take no action.
>
> 4) **Surrender to it** – just give up and give in.

James gives us some extreme examples of what causes conflict and what happens when it is not dealt with in the right way:

What causes quarrels and what causes fights among you? Is it not this, that your passions are at war within you? You desire and do not have, so you murder. You covet and cannot obtain, so you fight and quarrel. **– James 4:1-2a (ESV)**

I think we're all aware of what conflict is, and how destructive it can be. So let's spend the rest of our time together learning how to remove the mask of conflict from our lives. What should I do when I find myself in conflict with someone else? How do I remove the mask?

1. BRING THE CONFLICT TO GOD

Philippians 4:6-7

1 Peter 5:6-7

2. TAKE A DEEP LOOK WITHIN MYSELF

Matthew 7:3-4

3. ALLOW GOD TO DO HIS WORK IN ME

1 Peter 1:6-7

4. FORGIVE ANY WRONGS AND MOVE ON

Matthew 18:21-22

Take Off Your Mask:
"Controlling the Chaos"

Introduction:

[9]In March of 2009, the police department of Dallas, Texas, joined a growing number of agencies getting rid of complicated codes used in radio calls or signals. Instead, operators and officers now communicate through a plain-language system that relies on ordinary words and phrases.

For example, in the past an officer might have radioed in to say, "I'm approaching a Code 7 on Highland Ave." Now they just say, "I'm approaching a minor accident on Highland."

The switch is due in large part to the terrorist attacks of September 11, 2001. During the chaos that resulted from the attacks, many federal agencies and officers had trouble communicating with each other because they used different codes for different situations—or worse, similar codes that had different meanings between agencies. As a result of that confusion, federal officials mandated that plain-language be used when police and other federal agents respond to major disasters. Many local police and fire departments have followed suit in recent years.

Herb Ebsen, a senior corporal with the Dallas Police Department, thinks the change to a plain-language system is a great idea. "It's just common sense," he said. "If we start speaking in codes, you have a real chance for a problem or misinterpretation."

I wonder if something similar would work with our chaotic lives? Many of us have so many things going on at once that we don't know whether we are coming or going. Is there a way to make things less complicated? Is there a way to find peace?

---

[9] ERIC AASEN, "DALLAS POLICE DEPARTMENT DROPPING POLICE CODE FOR PLAIN ENGLISH," WWW.DALLASNEWS.COM (3-23-10)

We are continuing our series today, "Take Off Your Mask." Our key verse is 2 Corinthians 4:2 from "The Message" paraphrase:

We refuse to wear masks and play games. We don't maneuver and manipulate behind the scenes. And we don't twist God's Word to suit ourselves. Rather, we keep everything we do and say out in the open, the whole truth on display, so that those who want to can see and judge for themselves in the presence of God. – **2 Corinthians 4:2 (MSG)**

One of the masks we wear is in this area of chaos. When our lives become chaotic we tend to become scattered, reactive, frantic, or stressed. And in the world we live in that is not hard to do. It begins to wear on us, and we wear a mask that says everything is okay on the outside, but we might be falling apart on the inside.

"But watch yourselves lest your hearts be weighed down with dissipation and drunkenness and cares of this life, and that day come upon you suddenly like a trap." – **Luke 21:34 (ESV)**

There is not a person in this room that has not dealt with the cares of this life. Some are more serious than others, but we all face situations that we do not know how to deal with, do not want to deal with, and wish that they would somehow go away. I want us to take a few moments to consider the peace God offers to us in our times of chaos by examining three specific areas where we can turn in times of struggle.

1. CONTROL THE CHAOS WITH GOD'S PROMISE OF PEACE

John 16:33

Matthew 6:34

2. CONTROL THE CHAOS WITH GOD'S PERSON OF PEACE

Romans 5:1-2

Isaiah 26:3

3. CONTROL THE CHAOS WITH GOD'S POWER OF PEACE

1) The Power of Intimacy with God

2 Thessalonians 3:16

2) The Power of Mental and Emotional Stability

Philippians 4:6-7

3) The Power of Christian Community

Ephesians 4:2-3

Take Off Your Mask:
"Bringing Light to Darkness"

Introduction:

We are continuing our series today we are calling, "Take Off Your Mask." The idea is that many people masquerade as something they really are not, or pretend things don't bother them that do, or act like they believe something they really do not, or twist things to fit someone else's perception. In other words, there are masks that all of us wear, and when we wear these masks we are not being honest with ourselves, with those around us, or with God.

One of the masks we wear is in the area of living in darkness. We often pretend that we are always walking in the light of Jesus Christ, but truth be told, we often find ourselves resorting to the person we were before we knew Him.

This is the message we have heard from him and proclaim to you, that God is light, and in him is no darkness at all. If we say we have fellowship with him while we walk in darkness, we lie and do not practice the truth. But if we walk in the light, as he is in the light, we have fellowship with one another, and the blood of Jesus his Son cleanses us from all sin. If we say we have no sin, we deceive ourselves, and the truth is not in us. If we confess our sins, he is faithful and just to forgive us our sins and to cleanse us from all unrighteousness. If we say we have not sinned, we make him a liar, and his word is not in us. – **1 John 1:5-10 (ESV)**

Once Paul the apostle was speaking before King Agrippa and he recounted for the King how Jesus had once appeared to him on the road to Damascus and this is what Jesus said to him:

"I am going to send you to the Gentiles, to open their eyes so they may turn from darkness to light, and from the power of Satan to God. Then they will receive forgiveness for their sins and be given a place among God's people, who are set apart by faith in me." – **Acts 26:17b-18 (ESV)**

Jesus is talking here about a dynamic change that will take place in the lives of those who trust in Him as their Savior and Lord. He is telling us plainly and clearly how we can take off our mask and walk in the light.

1. WE NEED TO MOVE FROM SATAN TO GOD

to open their eyes so they may turn...from the power of Satan to God.

> 2 Corinthians 4:4a

> Ephesians 2:2

> Luke 11:20-22

2. WE NEED TO MOVE FROM DARKNESS TO LIGHT

to open their eyes so they may turn from darkness to light...

> 2 Corinthians 4:4

> John 8:12

3. WE NEED TO MOVE FROM SELF TO SERVICE

> Luke 9:23-24

4. WE NEED TO MOVE FROM THE WORLD TO GOD'S KINGDOM

... they will... be given a place among God's people...

> Galatians 1:4

> Colossians 1:13

> Hebrews 13:14

> Philippians 3:20

Take Off Your Mask:
"Valuing What Matters"

Introduction:

We are continuing our series today we are calling, "Take Off Your Mask." The idea is that many people masquerade as something they really are not, or pretend things don't bother them that do, or act like they believe something they really do not, or twist things to fit someone else's perception.

One of the masks we wear is in the area of what we value. We often pretend that spiritual riches are what motivate us, but somehow we keep returning to the value of the almighty dollar.

But those who desire to be rich fall into temptation, into a snare, into many senseless and harmful desires that plunge people into ruin and destruction. For the love of money is a root of all kinds of evils. It is through this craving that some have wandered away from the faith and pierced themselves with many pangs. – **1 Timothy 6:9-10 (ESV)**

The solution to removing this mask is learning how to view money in the same way that God does, and to realize that everything we have is God's. The best way to cure ourselves of the love of money is to give our money back to God who gave it to us in the first place.

The point is this: whoever sows sparingly will also reap sparingly, and whoever sows bountifully will also reap bountifully. Each one must give as he has decided in his heart, not reluctantly or under compulsion, for God loves a cheerful giver. And God is able to make all grace abound to you, so that having all sufficiency in all things at all times, you may abound in every good work. As it is written, "He has distributed freely, he has given to the poor; his righteousness endures forever." He who supplies seed to the sower and bread for food will supply and multiply your seed for sowing and increase the harvest of your righteousness. You will be enriched in every way to be generous in every way, which through us will produce thanksgiving to God. – **2 Corinthians 9:6-11 (ESV)**

What we want to do today is learn a practical way that we can give the way that God wants us to so that we can take off our mask. There are three simple steps that we each need to take.

1. WE NEED TO THINK LIKE GODLY SERVANTS

Luke 16:13

1) Understand God's Ownership

Acts 17:25

1 Timothy 6:7

1 Chronicles 29:14

2) Value God's Partnership

2. WE NEED TO ACT LIKE TRUSTED MANAGERS

1) I Earn God's Trust with My Heart

Matthew 6:21

2) I Manage God's Money with God's Plan

1 Corinthians 16:1-2

1. By Giving Regularly

2. By Giving Personally

3. By Giving Systematically

4. By Giving Proportionately

3. WE NEED TO LIVE LIKE PRECIOUS HEIRS

1) Our Father wants to Train Us

1 Timothy 6:18-19

2) Our Father wants to Provide for Us

1 Timothy 6:17

Living the Faith Life: "Faith Under Pressure"

Introduction:

[10]In an on-line article for *Leadership* journal, John Ortberg discusses how adverse situations are necessary for our spiritual growth. He writes:

Psychologist Jonathon Haidt had a hypothetical exercise: Imagine that you have a child, and for five minutes you're given a script of what will be that child's life. You get an eraser. You can edit it. You can take out whatever you want.

You read that your child will have a learning disability in grade school. Reading, which comes easily for some kids, will be laborious for yours.

In high school, your kid will make a great circle of friends; then one of them will die of cancer.

After high school this child will actually get into the college they wanted to attend. While there, there will be a car crash, and your child will lose a leg and go through a difficult depression.

A few years later, your child will get a great job—then lose that job in an economic downturn.

Your child will get married, but then go through the grief of separation.

You get this script for your child's life and have five minutes to edit it.

What would you erase?

---

[10] Condensed from, JOHN ORTBERG, "THE GOOD NEWS AMID THE BAD NEWS," LEADERJOURNAL.NET (3-9-09)

Wouldn't you want to take out all the stuff that would cause them pain?

I am part of a generation of adults called "helicopter parents," because we're constantly trying to swoop into our kid's educational life, relational life, sports life, etc., to make sure no one is mistreating them, no one is disappointing them. We want them to experience one unobstructed success after another.

One Halloween a mom came to our door to trick or treat. Why didn't she send in her kid? Well, the weather's a little bad, she said; she was driving so he didn't have to walk in the mist.

But why not send him to the door? He had fallen asleep in the car, she said, so she didn't want him to have to wake up.

I felt like saying, "Why don't you eat all his candy and get his stomach ache for him, too—then he can be completely protected!"

If you could wave a wand, if you could erase every failure, setback, suffering, and pain—are you sure it would be a good idea? Would it cause your child to grow up to be a better, stronger, more generous person? Is it possible that in some way people actually need adversity, setbacks, maybe even something like trauma to reach the fullest level of development and growth?

As we begin our series, *Living the Faith-Life*, we will be looking at some important passages in the book of James, and today we are focused on James 1:1-12 and how to live with *Faith Under Pressure*. That pressure comes in all kinds of forms, but I think they mainly fall under the heading – *The Trials of Life* – We all have them, but how do we deal with them? Do we need a big eraser to remove them, or is there a better way?

1. ACCEPT GOD'S JOY

James 1:2-3

2. ACCEPT GOD'S GROWTH

James 1:4

3. ACCEPT GOD'S WISDOM

James 1:5-8

4. ACCEPT GOD'S GIFT

James 1:9-12

Living the Faith Life: "Faith in Action"

Introduction:

When we were traveling through the State of Missouri I noticed they had license plates that say "Show-Me State" on them. After inquiring about what this means I found out that the residents of Missouri are known for demanding proof before they will believe something. If I didn't know better I'd say that James was from Missouri. Because James isn't satisfied with someone simply saying they have faith, he wants them to show it.

What good is it, my brothers, if someone says he has faith but does not have works? Can that faith save him? If a brother or sister is poorly clothed and lacking in daily food, and one of you says to them, "Go in peace, be warmed and filled," without giving them the things needed for the body, what good is that? So also faith by itself, if it does not have works, is dead. But someone will say, "You have faith and I have works." Show me your faith apart from your works, and I will show you my faith by my works. You believe that God is one; you do well. Even the demons believe—and shudder! Do you want to be shown, you foolish person, that faith apart from works is useless? Was not Abraham our father justified by works when he offered up his son Isaac on the altar? You see that faith was active along with his works, and faith was completed by his works; and the Scripture was fulfilled that says, "Abraham believed God, and it was counted to him as righteousness"—and he was called a friend of God. You see that a person is justified by works and not by faith alone. And in the same way was not also Rahab the prostitute justified by works when she received the messengers and sent them out by another way? For as the body apart from the spirit is dead, so also faith apart from works is dead. – **James 2:14-26 (ESV)**

There are two main truths here concerning faith we need to consider:

1. SHOW ME FAITH

James gives four reasons why there is no profit to this kind of faith.

1) A mere profession of faith cannot save the sinner.

James 2:14

Ephesians 2:8-10

2) A mere profession of faith doesn't help others.

Matthew 25:41

3) A mere profession of faith doesn't have a shred of evidence as to its reality.

4) A mere profession of faith is no better than the faith of demons.

James 2:19

Matthew 8:29

Luke 4:34

2. SAVING FAITH

James 2:21-24

1) Abraham trusted God.

2) Abraham obeyed God.

Living the Faith Life: "Faith Under Control"

Introduction:

[11]Rabbi Joseph Telushkin, author of Words That Hurt, Words That Heal, has lectured throughout this country on the powerful, often negative impact of words. He often asks audiences if they can go 24 hours without saying any unkind words about, or to, another person. Invariably, a small number of listeners raise their hands, signifying "Yes." Others laugh, and quite a few call out, "No!"

Telushkin responds: "Those who can't answer 'yes' must recognize that you have a serious problem. If you can't go 24 hours without drinking liquor, you're addicted to alcohol. If you can't go 24 hours without smoking, you're addicted to nicotine. So if you can't go 24 hours without saying unkind words about others, then you've lost control over your tongue."

Many of us are in need of self-control when it comes to the use of our tongues. In many ways our tongues are more dangerous than any gun on street. Today we're going to examine the power of the tongue so that we'll be better able to identify the times when we're using ours in the wrong way and be able to exercise tongue control.

Not many of you should become teachers, my brothers, for you know that we who teach will be judged with greater strictness. For we all stumble in many ways. And if anyone does not stumble in what he says, he is a perfect man, able also to bridle his whole body. If we put bits into the mouths of horses so that they obey us, we guide their whole bodies as well. Look at the ships also: though they are so large and are driven by strong winds, they are guided by a very small rudder wherever the will of the pilot directs. So also the tongue is a small member, yet it boasts of great things. How great a forest is set ablaze by such a small fire! And the tongue is a fire, a world of unrighteousness. The tongue is set among our members, staining the whole body, setting on fire the entire course of life, and

---

[11] MARK MITCHELL, "THE LIFE-GIVING TONGUE," *Qoheleth* BLOG (11-15-13)

---

set on fire by hell. For every kind of beast and bird, of reptile and sea creature, can be tamed and has been tamed by mankind, but no human being can tame the tongue. It is a restless evil, full of deadly poison. With it we bless our Lord and Father, and with it we curse people who are made in the likeness of God. From the same mouth come blessing and cursing. My brothers, these things ought not to be so. Does a spring pour forth from the same opening both fresh and salt water? Can a fig tree, my brothers, bear olives, or a grapevine produce figs? Neither can a salt pond yield fresh water. – **James 3:1-12 (ESV)**

1. THE POWER TO DISCREDIT

Matthew 12:36

Those of you who are teachers need to be very careful what you say. There are two things you need to avoid that will discredit you and God:

1) Words that are Untrue.

Psalm 15:1-2

2) Words that are Unkind.

2. THE POWER TO DIRECT

3. THE POWER TO DESTROY

Proverbs 16:27

4. THE POWER TO DISPLAY

James 3:10

Living the Faith Life: "Faith That Submits"

Introduction:

One of the most successful coaches in professional football history was Vince Lombardi. Winner of the first two official Super Bowls, Lombardi established himself as a winner. Part of his secret was his ability to develop the right game plan. On the week of the game, Vince would meet with the quarterbacks on Wednesday, Thursday, and Friday to refine the game plan for Sunday. He went over every detail, covered every contingency, and left nothing to chance. By the close of the Friday meeting, the quarterbacks understood the game plan so perfectly they were prepared for anything that could happen. Bart Starr, Lombardi's starting quarterback, said he went into the game each week knowing he would never face any situation he was not equipped to handle. Lombardi had developed the perfect game plan, had communicated that to his team leaders, and they carried it out explicitly. The result was victory.

The Bible says we Christians are in a conflict with the principalities and powers of this world. Every day we do battle against these enemies who want to defeat us. We are in a struggle with the devil as we seek to further the kingdom of God and as he seeks to defeat the kingdom of God. How are we going to be victorious in this conflict against the devil? How are we going to win the victory in the game of life?

The good news for us is that the Bible gives us a game plan for fighting against the powers of this world, a game plan which if properly carried out will lead to personal victory. And if we are to be committed to Christ and His Church we must also be committed to His game plan so that we will be prepared for every contingency as we seek to win the battle for our Lord.

But he gives more grace. Therefore it says, "God opposes the proud, but gives grace to the humble." Submit yourselves therefore to God. Resist the devil, and he will flee from you. Draw near to God, and he will draw near to you. Cleanse your hands, you sinners, and purify your hearts, you double-minded. Be wretched and mourn and weep. Let your laughter be turned to mourning and your joy to gloom. Humble yourselves before the Lord, and he will exalt you. Do not speak evil against one another, brothers. The one who speaks against a brother or judges his brother, speaks evil against the law and judges the law. But if you judge the law, you are not a doer of the law but a judge. There is only one lawgiver and judge, he who is able to save and to destroy. But who are you to judge your neighbor? – **James 4:6-12 (ESV)**

1. SUBMISSION

1) The Proud.

2) The Humble.

2. OPPOSITION

1) He is Real.

2) He is Rebellious.

1. He lies

2. He Tempts

3. He is Relentless

1 Peter 5:8

3. COOPERATION

James 4:11-12

To criticize and slander one another is wrong for three reasons:

1) It is an infringement on love.

2) It is an infringement on God.

3) It is an infringement on others.

Living the Faith Life: "Faith That Prays"

Introduction:

Ace Collins told the following story about his friend's answered prayer:

[12]In the winter of 2007, a close friend of mine was felled by not one but two brain aneurysms. For weeks she lingered on life support, growing weaker each day. As her condition deteriorated, her children were called in to say their goodbyes, and her church prepared for a funeral. Then Linda suddenly snapped out of her coma. As she came to, she looked over at her husband and asked, "Where is everybody else?"

Shaking his head, he explained, "They allow only one of us at a time in the ICU. There is no one else here."

Linda argued, "No, I heard them. They were all speaking at the same time, and there were hundreds of them, too. Some of them I knew; others I didn't. But they were all around me. They were here!"

Linda's husband assured her that all those people had never been in the room. Like many, he initially thought that Linda must have been hallucinating. Some people speculated that Linda had seen and heard angels. But the real answer was probably much closer to home.

A few days after her miraculous recovery, Linda discovered that a large prayer chain had been created to pray for her. This group had been formed when news of her condition was sent out to local churches, and then it had spread to other groups throughout the region. Within days Linda's name had been placed on hundreds of prayer lists and written in scores of prayer logs. For weeks, thousands were praying for her each day. Her miraculous recovery convinced Linda of two things: the voices she heard were of the

---

[12] ACE COLLINS, *Sticks and Stones* (ZONDERVAN, 2009), PP. 207-208

people who had been praying for her, and those prayers had pulled her back from death's door.

Linda's story is far from unusual. Countless people have been touched by the power of prayer. Science and personal experiences have proven that the words of prayer do have impact. But that impact can't happen unless the ones doing the praying believe their words carry weight.

James teaches us that not only is this possible, but it is probable for people who really have faith that God will answer them. Let's look at three components of prayer that will help us in our own spiritual journey.

1. PRAISE

James 5:13

Ephesians 5:19

1 Corinthians 14:26

Colossians 3:16

2. PETITION

James 5:17

Matthew 17:20

1) Pray when you are suffering.

James 5:13

2) Pray when you are sick.

James 5:14-15

Notice that James gives a 3-part solution to the person who is afflicted.

1. Call for the elders of the church

2. The elders are to anoint the person with oil

3. The elders are to pray over the sick person

3) Pray when someone needs healing.

James 5:16

4) Pray when someone has turned from Christ.

James 5:19-20

3. CONFESSION

James 5:16

1 Timothy 2:5

1) Confession should generally be made to an individual.

2) Confession should be made to the person we sinned against.

Matthew 5:23-24

3) Confession should be made to a mature Christian if our sin is not against a person.

4) Confession should be understood, not as a law, but as a divinely given help to be practiced as God directs.

Living the Faith Life:
"Faithful in Caring for Us"

Introduction:

The Secret Service, a part of the Treasury Department, employs 4,300 people to protect the president and to safeguard the nation's money supply. In order to give the president constant protection, these agents stick extremely close to him wherever he goes. When he's walking, when he's riding in his limousine, when he's on vacation at a ski slope or a lake, the Secret Service is there, surrounding him, jogging by his car, skiing or fishing right beside him. If the president goes scuba diving, agents put on masks and tanks and go with him under the water.

Wouldn't it be nice to have someone who would always be with you, protect you, and help you — not out of duty, but just because they cared for you? Joshua knew God to be just such a friend as he stood at the border of Canaan, ready to lead the people of Israel into the Promised Land. In the passage before us, God makes the greatest promise of all: "I will be with you."

As we begin our new series "God is Faithful" let's find out what God means by this wonderful promise:

After the death of Moses the servant of the LORD, the LORD said to Joshua the son of Nun, Moses' assistant, "Moses my servant is dead. Now therefore arise, go over this Jordan, you and all this people, into the land that I am giving to them, to the people of Israel. Every place that the sole of your foot will tread upon I have given to you, just as I promised to Moses. From the wilderness and this Lebanon as far as the great river, the river Euphrates, all the land of the Hittites to the Great Sea toward the going down of the sun shall be your territory. No man shall be able to stand before you all the days of your life. Just as I was with Moses, so I will be with you. I will not leave you or forsake you. Be strong and courageous, for you shall cause this people to inherit the land that I swore to their fathers to give them. Only be strong and very courageous, being careful to do according to all the law that Moses my servant commanded you. Do not turn from it to the right hand or to the left, that you may have good success wherever you go. This Book of the Law shall not depart from your mouth, but you shall meditate on it day and night, so that you may be careful to do according to all that is written in it. For then you will make your way prosperous, and then you will have good success. Have I not commanded you? Be strong and courageous. Do not be frightened, and do not be dismayed, for the LORD your God is with you wherever you go." – **Joshua 1:1-9 (ESV)**

1. GOD'S CARING BRINGS US STRENGTH AND COURAGE

Deuteronomy 31:6

2. GOD'S CARING BRINGS US COMFORT

Psalm 139:7-12

Psalm 9:9

Psalm 121:5-8

Psalm 34:18

Psalm 37:24

Psalm 37:24

3. GOD'S CARING DEMANDS OUR OBEDIENCE

Joshua 1:7

1 Corinthians 15:57

Joshua 1:8a

God is Faithful: "Faithful in Our Trials"

Introduction: [Note: Read Lamentations 3:1-26]

When Helen Keller was only 18 months old, she lost her sight and hearing because of a severe illness. Until the age of six, she was the selfish center of the Keller household, and everything sympathetically revolved around her. Then Anne Sullivan, a 21-year-old graduate of the Perkins Institution for the Blind, arrived in Tuscumbia, AL, from Boston. Anne was there to open up Helen's world. But the trials Helen put her teacher through are legendary — the wrestling matches over the utensils Helen refused to use; the tug-of-war battles between Anne and the Keller family over Helen's welfare; and the sneaking attacks from the fighting, biting, unmanageable Helen. But Anne's patience and faithfulness to Helen paid off. Not only did Anne give Helen the gift of language, but she accompanied Helen throughout her entire education, including an exemplary college program in which Anne would read books "into Helen's hand" on many late nights so Helen's course work wouldn't be hindered. Helen Keller became an ambassador for the blind and the deaf and a monument to the heights a human can reach. In her 2nd auto-biography Helen wrote that Anne "was a delightful companion, entering into all my discoveries with the joy of a fellow explorer...Above all she loved me...By the vitalizing power of her friendship she has stirred and enlarged my faculties." The book's dedication reads simply: "To Anne Sullivan, whose love is the story of my life." Anne Sullivan was faithful to Helen Keller through trials, around obstacles, and over mountains that would have stopped Helen's successful pilgrimage through life.

You know God, in an even much greater way than Anne Sullivan, wants to be our faithful friend through all of our trials. In fact, the Bible plainly shows how God, the faithful One, is always there for His friends, even in the midst of great trials and suffering. By examining the causes of our trials and the choices we can make regarding them, I want us to learn how God will remain our faithful friend, even in the worst of times. Let's begin by considering:

1. THE CAUSES OF OUR TRIALS

James 1:2

Grief – Ruth 1:20-21

Stress – Numbers 11:15

Disaster

Fear – 2 Corinthians 1:8b

Frustration

Oppression – Psalm 42:9

Sickness – Isaiah 38:10

2. THE CHOICES WE CAN MAKE

1) Take our lives.

Job 2:9

Matthew 27:5

2) Try to ignore it.

3) Blame God for it.

4) Trust God in it.

2 Chronicles 15:2b

3. THE COMFORTS GOD OFFERS

1) Hope in remembrance.

Lamentations 3:21

Lamentations 3:22a

3) Compassion that never leaves us.

Lamentations 3:22b-23

4) Patience in waiting.

Lamentations 3:24-26

5) Ability to help others.

2 Corinthians 1:3-4

God is Faithful:
"Faithful in Our Temptations"

Introduction:

In John Bunyan's *Pilgrim's Progress*, a man named Christian is making his way from this world to the next, encountering pitfalls, dangers, and monsters along the way. The Slough of Despond, Apollyon, Vanity Fair, Doubting Castle, and Dark River are just a few of the obstacles that stood in the path of his journey.

For example, as Christian passes by a hill called Lucre, a man named Demas beckons and offers the riches of his silver mine. Christian hurries past, realizing the danger, but others immediately take the invitation of Demas, to their great regret. As they greedily climb up to look into the mine, they lose their footing and fall into the pit where they sink into the depths.

Christian escaped the temptations that swallowed others because he obeyed the words of the Great Book that started his journey. That Book tells us that we too, can escape temptation because God, our friend, is with us on our journey.

No temptation has overtaken you that is not common to man. God is faithful, and he will not let you be tempted beyond your ability, but with the temptation he will also provide the way of escape, that you may be able to endure it. – **1 Corinthians 10:13 (ESV)**

As we contemplate God's faithfulness in our temptations it will be helpful for us to consider three aspects of temptation.

1. THE CERTAINTY OF TEMPTATION

No temptation has overtaken you that is not common to man.

1) Temptation is common to Man.

1 Corinthians 10:1-5

Lust — 1 Corinthians 10:6

Idolatry —1 Corinthians 10:7

Sexual Immorality —1 Corinthians 10:8

Unbelief —1 Corinthians 10:9

Grumbling —1 Corinthians 10:10

2) Temptation is common to Christ.

Hebrews 4:15

2. THE CHARACTER OF TEMPTATION

1 Corinthians 10:13b

1 Corinthians 10:12

3. THE CONQUEST OF TEMPTATION

1 Corinthians 10:13c

1) Turn from Self.

Romans 7:18

2) Turn to Christ.

"God will provide the way of escape."

2 Corinthians 2:14a

God is Faithful: "Faithful to His Promises"

Introduction:

One of the most devastating lessons a young person learns is that people break their promises. Children naively assume that if someone says, "I promise," they can count on it. But this assumption takes a vicious beating.

A father vows to go camping with his son, but weekend after weekend finds Dad too busy with other matters. A mother pledges to take her daughter to the zoo, then forgets all about it. A child shares a secret with a friend, only to discover that everyone in his or her class at school is in on it.

No doubt you can give examples of promises made to you that were never kept. But God is able to keep His promises, no matter how unlikely their fulfilment may seem. Take the case of Abraham in Old Testament book of Genesis. He was nearly 100-years-old when the Lord renewed His pledge to give him a son. The patriarch's wife, Sarah, was 90. Romans 4:18-21 gives us Abraham's response to this seemingly impossible promise:

In hope he believed against hope, that he should become the father of many nations, as he had been told, "So shall your offspring be." He did not weaken in faith when he considered his own body, which was as good as dead (since he was about a hundred years old), or when he considered the barrenness of Sarah's womb. No unbelief made him waver concerning the promise of God, but he grew strong in his faith as he gave glory to God, fully convinced that God was able to do what he had promised. – Romans 4:18-21 (ESV)

Abraham was not the only person in the Old Testament who recognized God's ability to keep His promises. Joshua wrote:

Not one word of all the good promises that the LORD had made to the house of Israel had failed; all came to pass. – Joshua 21:45 (ESV)

And later he told the people of Israel:

"And now I am about to go the way of all the earth, and you know in your hearts and souls, all of you, that not one word has failed of all the good things that the LORD your God promised concerning you. All have come to pass for you; not one of them has failed." – **Joshua 23:14 (ESV)**

A few hundred years later King Solomon reminded his generation of the same thing when he said in 1 Kings 8:56:

"Blessed be the LORD who has given rest to his people Israel, according to all that he promised. Not one word has failed of all his good promise, which he spoke by Moses his servant." – **1 Kings 8:56 (ESV)**

Yes, the Bible gives ample proof of God's ability to keep His promises, even when they seem incredible. Yet most of us have difficulty believing our Lord can calm our emotions or silence the worries that nag at our hearts. Unlike Abraham, we do not feel completely assured that what God has promised He is also able to perform.

1. WHAT ARE GOD'S PROMISES?

1) God promises the Holy Spirit to people who have put their faith in Christ.

Ephesians 1:13

2) God promises an abundant life that will never end.

1 John 5:11-12

John 10:28

3) God promises us spiritual rest.

Hebrews 4:1

Hebrews 3:19

2 Corinthians 1:20

2. WHY ARE GOD'S PROMISES TRUE?

1) God is Truthful.

Titus 1:2

Romans 15:8

2) God is Trustworthy.

Hebrews 10:23b

3. HOW DO WE RECEIVE GOD'S PROMISES?

1) Prayerful Study of Scripture.

2) Patiently Waiting.

Hebrews 6:15

3) Obedience to God's Will.

Hebrews 10:36

4) Faith.

Romans 4:20

Philippians 4:7

James 1:5

1 John 1:9

A Brand New You: "Renewed by the Spirit"

Introduction:

A church in Naperville, Illinois, in the western suburbs of Chicago is boasting new bells in their belfry. Since the church was built two decades ago, the congregation has held off on its plans to hang bells in a large open space above the sanctuary. Due to limited funds, the congregation suggested mounting a cross in the space or a series of liturgical banners that could be hung according to the seasons of the church year. In conjunction with the church's 25th anniversary, the church finally found the means to spring for three bells to fill the vacant hole – They are beautiful.

However, you'll never hear these bells peal on Sunday mornings (or any other day of the week for that matter). And it doesn't have to do with city ordinances or complaining neighbors opposed to bells playing hymns. It has to do with the fact that the bells aren't real – they don't have clappers. Although they look authentic, they are made of resin.

At some point in our lives, most Christ Followers can relate to those bells. We look, say, and do things that are representative of our faith, yet deep inside we no longer sense the power of God living inside of us.

Over the next few weeks I'll be preaching on *A Brand New You: Becoming the Person You Were Created to Be* because I sense that a lot of us are in need of a do-over. We need a fresh injection of the power of God in our lives so that we can accomplish what He has called us to as a church and individuals. And the place that we really need to start is with a renewal of the Holy Spirit in our lives. I want us to do some soul-searching today by considering three questions that are vital to Holy Spirit renewal in our lives. The first question we need to consider is this:

1. DO I NEED HOLY SPIRIT RENEWAL?

1) Am I eager to serve God?

Romans 7:6

2) Am I enjoying time with God?

Romans 14:17-18

3) Am I growing in relationship with God?

1 Peter 2:2

4) Am I a Godly example for others?

1 Corinthians 11:1

2. HOW CAN I BE RENEWED?

Colossians 3:10

1) Renew my commitment

Psalm 51:8, 10

2) Surrender my will

Romans 8:9

Ephesians 5:18

3) Live in obedience

John 14:15

Galatians 5:16

Galatians 5:25

A Brand New You: "Renewed by our Vision"

Introduction:

Today is our second message in the series – *A Brand New You: Becoming the Person You Were Created to Be.* Today we want to focus on our need to renew our vision for Christ and for His Church.

Most of you will remember when you first became a Christian that you were fired up with a vision to reach people for Christ and to see His Church grow. You probably spent considerable time in prayer asking God to use you for His kingdom and to make you a strong witness to others. You saw yourself as a champion for Christ, proclaiming victory in His Name and defeating the enemy with the sword of the Spirit. When you heard sermons about evangelism and outreach, you got fired up and clearly understood and accepted the fact that God could use you in a mighty way.

But somehow, over the years, or months since your conversion to Christ, somehow that vision has faded and become nothing more than a distant memory. You might still talk about it, and you know it's something that should be important to you – but if the truth be known, it's the last thing on your mind these days.

Think about this for a minute – in this last week, how much time did you spend pondering the fact that God has a vision for your life and for this church? If you're like most people, you probably gave it little, if any, thought. I want to try and help us change that today by letting you in on something – you are an integral part of God's plan for this world. And God wants to give you the ability to fulfill that plan in your life and in your church.

God wants us to begin thinking on a much grander scale than we've been thinking, and bring to us a personal renewal that focuses on a vision for the future. There are three sentences on your outline that we're going to complete together.

1. GOD SAYS THAT...I AM COMMISSIONED

Matthew 28:18-20

...I am empowered.

Acts 1:8

...I am entrusted.

1 Thessalonians 2:4

2. I NEED TO...SEE MYSELF AS GOD SEES ME

...Realize that I am one part of the whole.

Romans 12:4-5

...Encourage vision in others.

3. WITH MY PARTICIPATION...

...Our church will grow spiritually.

...Our church will grow numerically.

...Our church will grow financially.

A Brand New You:
"Renewed by our Thinking"

Introduction:

The average brain weighs about three pounds – it contains 12 billion cells. Each one of these cells is connected to 10,000 other brain cells, totaling 120 trillion brain connections. Dr. Duane Gish has observed that "the human brain is the most complex arrangement of matter in the universe." Some have compared the brain to a sophisticated computer, but technology still has a long way to go before it can duplicate the brain's capabilities.

The brain is not only the most complex mechanism in the world; it is the most influential organ in your body. It accounts for your ability to think, remember, love, hate, feel, reason, imagine and analyze. Everything we see, hear, touch and smell is recorded on the lobes of the brain.

Your brain elevates you high above the animal kingdom – it literally sustains your life. If you are brain dead, you *are* dead because the brain supervises everything you do from the involuntary beat of your heart to the conscious decisions of daily life. It also houses your intuition, your conscience and your sexuality. It both houses and actually constitutes the mind.

Proverbs 23:7 summarizes so well the over-arching significance of the mind as far as God is concerned in this poetic declaration:

For as he thinks within himself, so he is. – **Proverbs 23:7a (NASB)**

We may rightly conclude that the human mind is the single most important entity in Creation – for as it goes, so goes the person and the society in which he/she lives. Who and what we will be then must have its origin and sustenance in the mind. What we sanction or suppress mentally determines whether we take the high road less traveled or the low road which is far more popular.

The degree to which we attain the mind of Christ will determine the quality of life we enjoy as well as the eternity we will experience. When we train our minds to become like the mind of Christ Himself we will find ourselves well on the way to personal renewal, because we will begin to think, act and do things like Jesus Himself.

Do not be conformed to this world, but be transformed by the renewal of your mind, that by testing you may discern what is the will of God, what is good and acceptable and perfect. – **Romans 12:2 (ESV)**

The point of this is simple – the pattern of conformity to the world is broken and a person's life is transformed only *if and when* the mind is renewed. Whether this renewal of the mind will take place depends upon our daily mental discipline.

Unquestionably and repeatedly the thought life is identified in Scripture as the very source of godliness or worldliness; holiness or unholiness. Our thinking may be dominated by the Holy Spirit or the evil one. We make the determination – we give the permission – we exercise the control. Our thought life is the real battleground – it is in our thinking that the most basic spiritual struggle takes place.

In the Old Testament as well as the New, the government of the mind is the condition which brings about spiritual transformation at the deepest level of a person's being and determines whether we are holy and pleasing to God. There are two basic areas that we need to really concentrate on today, so that we can truly experience *A Brand New You.*

THE GOAL: OBTAIN THE MIND OF CHRIST

1. I NEED TO KNOW CHRIST

1 Corinthians 2:16

1 Corinthians 2:14

2. I NEED TO SURRENDER CONTROL

Romans 8:6

3. I NEED TO WAGE WAR WITH EVIL

Romans 7:23-25

THE OUTCOME: A BRAND NEW YOU

1. SATAN IS DEFEATED

2. GUILT IS REMOVED

Psalm 19:13

3. GOD'S WILL IS DISCERNED

How Did They Do It?:
"They Lived in Expectancy"

Introduction:

Today we begin a new series looking at the early church in Acts and the amazing things they were able to accomplish. We are asking the question of them – "How did they do it?" and are hoping and praying that as we discover the answers we will be able to apply them to ourselves and our church so that we can accomplish similar things.

I think you would agree that some of the most exciting periods of our lives are times of anticipation. The times when we can't think of anything but what we are expecting to occur. I can remember many times like these: counting the days till Christmas; getting driver's license; marriage; and so on. When we are living with an attitude of expectancy our steps begin to quicken and our eyes brighten as we reach out to our future dreams.

When Jesus ascended from the Mount of Olives to His throne in glory, He left His church in an attitude of expectancy.

In the first book, O Theophilus, I have dealt with all that Jesus began to do and teach, until the day when he was taken up, after he had given commands through the Holy Spirit to the apostles whom he had chosen. He presented himself alive to them after his suffering by many proofs, appearing to them during forty days and speaking about the kingdom of God. And while staying with them he ordered them not to depart from Jerusalem, but to wait for the promise of the Father, which, he said, "you heard from me; for John baptized with water, but you will be baptized with the Holy Spirit not many days from now." So when they had come together, they asked him, "Lord, will you at this time restore the kingdom to Israel?" He said to them, "It is not for you to know times or seasons that the Father has fixed by his own authority. But you will receive power when the Holy Spirit has come upon you, and you will be my witnesses in Jerusalem and in all Judea and Samaria, and to the end of the

earth." And when he had said these things, as they were looking on, he was lifted up, and a cloud took him out of their sight. And while they were gazing into heaven as he went, behold, two men stood by them in white robes, and said, "Men of Galilee, why do you stand looking into heaven? This Jesus, who was taken up from you into heaven, will come in the same way as you saw him go into heaven."
Then they returned to Jerusalem from the mount called Olivet, which is near Jerusalem, a Sabbath day's journey away. And when they had entered, they went up to the upper room, where they were staying, Peter and John and James and Andrew, Philip and Thomas, Bartholomew and Matthew, James the son of Alphaeus and Simon the Zealot and Judas the son of James. All these with one accord were devoting themselves to prayer, together with the women and Mary the mother of Jesus, and his brothers. – **Acts 1:1-14 (ESV)**

Here in this last earthly meeting of Jesus and His disciples we find the Lord leaves them with a promise of something great that is going to take place in their lives. They are to wait for the baptism of the Holy Spirit that will empower them to be witnesses for Jesus to the world. Jesus left them in an attitude of expectancy.

We at (Name of Church) must also learn to have an attitude of expectancy. We must learn to:

1. WAIT WITH EXPECTANCY

Matthew 28:19

Acts 1:7

2. WATCH WITH EXPECTANCY

Matthew 24:42

Matthew 25:13

3. WORK WITH EXPECTANCY

Acts 1:11

How Did They Do It?:
"They Focused on Fellowship"

Introduction:

[13]A minister was once trying to talk to a man about coming to church. The man said he was a Christian, and the minister took him at his word. But when the minister urged the man to come to church, the man said that he could be just as good of a Christian alone.

They happened to be sitting in front of a wood stove that contained a coal fire. The minister took the tongs from beside the stove, reached in, and picked out one of the live coals. He carried it over to one side and laid it down on the stone slab, beside the stove he had removed it from. That single coal, which had been fiery red when it was in a group of burning coals turned gray and began to cool off.

Then the minister went over with the tongs, picked up that single piece of coal which had become gray and cold, and put it back in the center with the live coals. Soon it began to glow, and began to throw off light and heat once more.

This minister was trying to show this man that it is impossible to be on fire for the Lord without possessing an attitude of fellowship. Like the burning coal removed from the rest of the coals, a Christian who removes himself from the fellowship of the saints usually dies out and becomes cold in his/her faith. But the coals which remain in the fire are like a Christian who has an attitude of fellowship which is expressed by seeking every opportunity to be with his fellow saints.

The early church had a unity and effectiveness that is seldom seen today. As we ask, "How did they do it?" Let's look at Acts 2:42-47 to find our answer.

---

[13] Author unknown.

And they devoted themselves to the apostles' teaching and the fellowship, to the breaking of bread and the prayers. And awe came upon every soul, and many wonders and signs were being done through the apostles. And all who believed were together and had all things in common. And they were selling their possessions and belongings and distributing the proceeds to all, as any had need. And day by day, attending the temple together and breaking bread in their homes, they received their food with glad and generous hearts, praising God and having favor with all the people. And the Lord added to their number day by day those who were being saved.
– **Acts 2:42-47 (ESV)**

We notice these early Christians had a:

1. FELLOWSHIP OF WORSHIP

Acts 2:42

Acts 2:46-47

2. FELLOWSHIP OF WEALTH

Acts 2:44-45

Luke 16:11

3. FELLOWSHIP OF WITNESS

1) I care about numbers because God cares about numbers.

2) I care about numbers because when the numbers get higher it is a gauge we can use to demonstrate that our congregation is experiencing spiritual growth.

3) I care about numbers because every number that's recorded on our attendance board represents one of you sitting here today.

How Did They Do It?:
"They Cultivated Courage"

Introduction:

[Note to preacher – if you are not familiar with the ad mentioned below, please look at the last page of this sermon starter.]

Some of you probably remember the old advertisements in comic books for the Charles Atlas training course that would help you to gain a muscular physique. There was a skinny guy on the beach who gets sand kicked in his face by a bully, but there is nothing he can do – that is, until he gets the Charles Atlas course, gets buffed up, and returns to the beach to punch the bully in the face. I could always relate to guy getting sand kicked in his face, if only I'd buy the Charles Atlas course, maybe then I'd have courage.

In Acts 4 we find that the early church had cultivated an attitude of courage, but it didn't come from taking the Charles Atlas course. Let's read vv.1-31 together to see how they obtained the courage necessary to be bold in their witness for Christ.

[READ Acts 4:1-31]

To cultivate the courage we see in the early church there are four things we must do:

1. WE MUST BE FILLED WITH THE HOLY SPIRIT

Ephesians 5:18

2. WE MUST STAND ON JESUS' NAME

Acts 4:12

3. WE MUST PREACH THE RESURRECTION

Acts 4:2

Philippians 3:10a

2 Corinthians 5:17

4. WE MUST RELY ON THE POWER OF PRAYER

Acts 4:29-30

Acts 4:31

How Did They Do It?:
"They Emphasized Outreach"

Introduction:

Antioch was the least likely place to find the most powerful Christian fellowship of the 1st century. One of 16 cities by that name, Syrian Antioch, or Antioch-on-the-Orontes, was the 3rd city of the empire, ranked after Rome and Alexandria. It had a population of 500,000 people. Called "Antioch the Beautiful" it was the capital of the East. Cicero called it "renowned" and "populous," the "seat of brilliant scholarship and artistic refinement." Its colonnades, public baths, central plumbing and heating, and especially its resplendent lighting system made it one of the most modern cities of its day. It was an important trade center; it was also cosmopolitan, with large Jewish, Syrian, Greek, and Roman communities.

Antioch's citizens had gained a reputation for pleasure-seeking and low morals. Men everywhere knew them for their chariot races and sensuality. Located in this city was the Temple of Daphne. According to legend, Daphne, a mortal maid, attracted the attention of Apollo, the sun god. Daphne was turned into a laurel bush to preserve her from his pursuit. Worshippers and priestesses from the Temple of Daphne met in the laurel groves of the pleasure gardens 5 miles outside of Antioch to reenact the pursuit of Daphne by Apollo and to engage in ritual prostitution.

Yet, we find that in the midst of the paganism and prostitution the mighty Church of God arose. Acts 11 is a point of transition in the book of Acts. We see a transition from an emphasis on Peter to an emphasis on Paul. We see a transition from an emphasis on the Jews to an emphasis on Gentiles. And we see a transition from an emphasis on the Jerusalem church to an emphasis on the church at Antioch. From this point on, with the exclusion of Acts 15, the church at Antioch holds center stage throughout the book of Acts. Let's find out about it from Acts 11 and 13. READ 11:19-30; 13:1-3.

Now those who were scattered because of the persecution that arose over Stephen traveled as far as Phoenicia and Cyprus and Antioch, speaking the word to no one except Jews. But there were some of them, men of Cyprus and Cyrene, who on coming to Antioch spoke to the Hellenists also, preaching the Lord Jesus. And the hand of the Lord was with them, and a great number who believed turned to the Lord. The report of this came to the ears of the church in Jerusalem, and they sent Barnabas to Antioch. When he came and saw the grace of God, he was glad, and he exhorted them all to remain faithful to the Lord with steadfast purpose, for he was a good man, full of the Holy Spirit and of faith. And a great many people were added to the Lord. So Barnabas went to Tarsus to look for Saul, and when he had found him, he brought him to Antioch. For a whole year they met with the church and taught a great many people. And in Antioch the disciples were first called Christians. Now in these days prophets came down from Jerusalem to Antioch. And one of them named Agabus stood up and foretold by the Spirit that there would be a great famine over all the world (this took place in the days of Claudius). So the disciples determined, every one according to his ability, to send relief to the brothers living in Judea. And they did so, sending it to the elders by the hand of Barnabas and Saul. – **Acts 11:19-30 (ESV)**

Now there were in the church at Antioch prophets and teachers, Barnabas, Simeon who was called Niger, Lucius of Cyrene, Manaen a lifelong friend of Herod the tetrarch, and Saul. While they were worshiping the Lord and fasting, the Holy Spirit said, "Set apart for me Barnabas and Saul for the work to which I have called them." Then after fasting and praying they laid their hands on them and sent them off. – **Acts 13:1-3 (ESV)**

It is evident from these texts that the church at Antioch had an emphasis on outreach – an emphasis that we in the 21st century church would do well to imitate. Let's take some time today to discover what it was about this church that allowed them to look beyond themselves to a hurting world outside their doors.

1. AN EVANGELISTIC NATURE

Acts 11:21

2. A SOUND DOCTRINE

Acts 11:26a

3. A BOLD CHARACTER

Acts 11:26

4. A CARING ATTITUDE

Acts 11:29-30

5. A MISSIONARY SPIRIT

Living Like Jesus: "What Do We Need to Change to Live Like Jesus?"

Introduction:

In 1897, Charles Sheldon wrote a book titled, *In His Steps*. In it, he wrote about the mythical town of *Raymond* that experienced transformation because of church members who were challenged to a new commitment. Reverend Maxwell, the minister of the church, was preparing a sermon on 1 Peter 2:21.

For to this you have been called, because Christ also suffered for you, leaving you an example, so that you might follow in his steps. – **1 Peter 2:21 (ESV)**

The doorbell rang and the minister went to the door to discover a young man – a tramp, looking for work. He expressed his sympathy, but was unable to help the man who stood dejectedly at his door. Two hours later the minister's sermon was finished, and that Sunday he preached on the topic of: "The Sacrifice and Example of Christ."

At the end of the service, a man came to the front of the church and began giving a speech. The minister recognized him to be the same one whom he had seen the day before. "I'm not drunk ... and I'm not crazy," the young man began. "But I lost my job ten months ago. I'm a printer by trade and I've not been able to find work. My wife died four months ago and I have a little girl that I can't take care of. I don't expect you to find a job for me, but I do wonder what you mean when you say 'I'll go with Jesus all the way?' What does it mean when you sing songs like, 'Jesus, I My Cross Have Taken'? Are you folks actually denying yourself to win the lost? Are you making sacrifices to help people in distress?"

As the story goes, the man collapsed after his brief speech and was taken to the minister's home and cared for. He died later that week, and his last request was that he see his daughter, a request that was granted. His last words were, "Thank you for taking care of me ... I think this is what Jesus would have done."

The next Sunday, the minister gave a challenge to his congregation: How many would be willing to pledge themselves to this basic proposition – that for one full year they would do nothing without first asking "What would Jesus do?"

About 50 people were willing to take him up on his challenge. There was a publisher of a newspaper, a superintendent of the railway, school teachers, and a woman who had just inherited a million dollars. After the service, the minister explained that although they might not always know what Jesus would do in a particular situation, these people were committing themselves to asking the question and answering it as best they could. He also cautioned them not to make any decisions on the basis of immediate results. The real question was: What would Jesus do? Once that was answered, it was the responsibility of each person to obey.

The rest of Charles Sheldon's book addressed the struggles each person accepting the challenge faced in applying this basic question to his life. The publisher of a Sunday newspaper wondered whether Christ would have published a Sunday edition. He made some tough decisions without any regard to the consequences – whether the circulation would increase or decrease. Others found it difficult to apply this question to their lives, but as best as they knew how, they were obedient to Christ. As a result of asking this question, What would Jesus do? and trying their best to live out the answer, a revival came to that community.

You and I both know that our lives have become very complicated. We are cluttered and we are confused; we don't know what we should be doing. Could our lives be simplified merely by asking: What would Jesus do? How would He treat His employees? How would He invest His money? How would He spend His time?

Yes, on many occasions we might not know the answer to that question, but for each time we would be puzzled, we may have three or four times when we know perfectly well what Christ would do if He were in our shoes. "What would Jesus do?" If we took this question seriously, what would our priorities be? Let's think of it this way – What do we need to change to live like Jesus?"

1. WE NEED TO CHANGE WHAT WE THINK

Matthew 9:22

2. WE NEED TO CHANGE WHAT WE SAY

James 3:6

3. WE NEED TO CHANGE WHAT WE VALUE

1 Peter 2:21

Living Like Jesus: "With Jesus in the Desert"

Introduction:

In this series we are trying to understand and apply the question, "How do we live like Jesus did?" to our lives. If we could do this successfully, and I believe we can, it would certainly change many of our priorities, wouldn't it? If we had this question taped on our television sets, our checkbooks, on our phones and on our refrigerators, we would find that our lives would be dramatically changed.

When we study the life of Christ we find that central to everything that He did was His desert experience. He was well acquainted with the rugged terrain of Judea and the wastelands near the Jordan. That is where Christ walked, struggled and prayed. In the cities He did his work, but in the desert He received His power. If we are to follow in His steps, if we are to do what Jesus would do, we too must become acquainted with the desert. When we go through the desert with Christ, we find it represents several different places to us:

1. A PLACE OF CONFLICT

Luke 4:1-2

Luke 4:13

2. A PLACE OF COMMUNION

Luke 5:15-16

Luke 6:12

John 11:41-42

3. A PLACE OF COMMITMENT

Luke 22:40-42

4. A PLACE OF CONTENTMENT

Living Like Jesus:
"With Jesus in the Community"

Introduction:

What happens when Christ visits a community? In Luke 19 we have the story of Christ entering the city of Jericho. His entrance created a stir; people crowded around Him, trying to touch Him and hear His words. As we consider this passage today, we will be encouraged to remember that Christ visits us today, too; not in bodily form, but by His Holy Spirit. At least some of the same phenomena that happened back then, can happen today.

On at least three occasions, the United States has had a special visit from Christ, if I might be permitted to use such terminology. I'm thinking of the three great revivals – we call them the Great Awakenings. Usually, God waters the earth with a gentle rain, but sometimes He sends a cloudburst. That's what a revival is — the revitalization of the spiritual life of thousands of Christians simultaneously.

Remember that we have had such a special visit even in the twentieth century. In 1904 the news of the revival in Wales spilled over to the United States, generating much religious interest. For example, in Atlantic City, New Jersey one observer thought that nearly sixty thousand people had professed faith in Christ. In Newark, the secular press dedicated an entire column each day to what was happening in the churches. In Atlanta, one thousand businessmen united for intercession and, on November 2nd, stores and offices were closed at midday for prayer. In Louisville, Kentucky one man wrote, "The whole city is breathing a spiritual atmosphere – everywhere in shops and stores, in the mill and on the street, salvation is the sole topic of conversation."

But, perhaps the most striking example of revival occurred in Denver in 1905. On January 20th there was a day of prayer in the city, and by 10:00 in the morning churches were filled; by 11:30 almost all the stores were closed so people could pray; and at 12:00

noon four theaters had been designated by the mayor, and were filled for prayer.

In Portland, one writer says, "For three hours a day business was practically suspended; and from the crowds in the great department stores to the humblest clerk, from bank Presidents to boot blacks, all abandoned money-making for soul-saving."

That's what happens when Christ comes to town! And that's what happens when we come to town, following the example that Jesus has set for us. When God works mightily, people will know about it. Christ's visit to Jericho will serve as a backdrop to revival for us today. To remind us of what happens when Christ visits a community.

He entered Jericho and was passing through. And behold, there was a man named Zacchaeus. He was a chief tax collector and was rich. And he was seeking to see who Jesus was, but on account of the crowd he could not, because he was small in stature. So he ran on ahead and climbed up into a sycamore tree to see him, for he was about to pass that way. And when Jesus came to the place, he looked up and said to him, "Zacchaeus, hurry and come down, for I must stay at your house today." So he hurried and came down and received him joyfully. And when they saw it, they all grumbled, "He has gone in to be the guest of a man who is a sinner." And Zacchaeus stood and said to the Lord, "Behold, Lord, the half of my goods I give to the poor. And if I have defrauded anyone of anything, I restore it fourfold." And Jesus said to him, "Today salvation has come to this house, since he also is a son of Abraham. For the Son of Man came to seek and to save the lost." – **Luke 19:1-10 (ESV)**

When Christ visits a community:

1. THERE IS CURIOSITY

Luke 19:4

2. THERE IS CONFRONTATION

Luke 19:5

3. THERE IS CONFESSION

Luke 19:8

4. THERE IS CONVERSION

Luke 19:9-10

Living Like Jesus:
"With Jesus, Touching the Untouchable"

Introduction:

What would change in our lives if we decided to live like Jesus lived? There are many ways in which we cannot follow Christ, but in principle we can follow Him as He becomes involved with human need. One of the best ways for us to know whether we are following Christ is to ask whether we have had to make hard choices in His favor. That ultimately is the true nature of love; love makes sacrifices.

In Matthew 8, Christ encountered a leper. It's difficult for us to grasp the loathsomeness of leprosy in ancient times. The victim would experience lethargy and pain; after that, discolored patches would appear over his body. Then nodules (pink and brown) would ulcerate. These open sores would emit a foul discharge. The voice would become hoarse, the breath wheezing. Soon the victim's head would become so contorted that he scarcely looked human. Finally, there was a loss of sensation because the nerve trunks became affected. The muscles wasted away, and eventually the fingers and the toes would fall off. Most people lived an average of nine years after contracting the disease. Someone has rightly observed that leprosy made a human being a hideous wreck.

And what was the response of the people? In keeping with the Old Testament law, lepers were to be kept outside the camp. In Leviticus 13:45-46 we read:

"The leprous person who has the disease shall wear torn clothes and let the hair of his head hang loose, and he shall cover his upper lip and cry out, 'Unclean, unclean.' He shall remain unclean as long as he has the disease. He is unclean. He shall live alone. His dwelling shall be outside the camp." – **Leviticus 13:45-46 (ESV)**

Lepers were shunned and did not even have the right to speak to other human beings. They cried "Unclean! Unclean!" so that other people would not get near them. They always had to stand at a distance, and eventually die in their aloneness.

During the middle ages, a leper was brought into the church and the priest read the burial rights to him. Then a black garment was put upon him and he was avoided like the plague. He was considered dead, though he was still alive.

But let's consider our text and see how Jesus deals with a leper:

When he came down from the mountain, great crowds followed him. And behold, a leper came to him and knelt before him, saying, "Lord, if you will, you can make me clean." And Jesus stretched out his hand and touched him, saying, "I will; be clean." And immediately his leprosy was cleansed. – **Matthew 8:1-3 (ESV)**

1. THE CRY OF THOSE IN NEED

"Lord, if You will, You can make me clean."

2. THE CHURCH'S RESPONSIBILITY

And when I speak of "the church's responsibility" I mean all of us, both individually and corporately, who make up the church. First, we have a responsibility to those who were molested as children. They feel unclean, they do not like to be touched and they live with shame.

Then there are divorced people. Sometimes we are uncomfortable with them, because we know that someone is always guilty when a divorce takes place. But I've met a lot of innocent people out there who have been victims of bad marriages. I know of one woman who said that the Sunday after her divorce was finalized she came into church and felt as if she had a big "D" branded on her forehead. Some of you here today can relate to her. Divorced = Unclean in many people's eyes. Many of these people, particularly single parents, desperately need the love and the support of the church.

And what about those suffering from disease? There are many in our society who have various diseases and some of them are terminal. They need someone to come along and grant them comfort and let them know that Jesus loves them. They are in need of our love, our touch, and our compassion.

Dorie Van Stone told the story of a young man who just sat and stared after one of her seminars. When everyone else had left, he came up and said, "Dorie, I was thrown out on the street at the age of 9, my mother did not want me. I became a homosexual and contracted AIDS. A year ago, I became a Christian. Dorie, please tell me ... please tell me that I am forgiven! Tell me that I am forgiven!" She showed the young man passages of Scripture that assured him that he had been cleansed by Christ. And then she took him in her arms and held him as she would her own son. As his tears fell onto her sweater he said, "Dorie, nobody touches me ... some of my friends even think they could get AIDS through my tears." That's what Christ would have done.

Living Like Jesus: "We Can Do It!"

Introduction:

We can easily tell whether we are following Christ by answering two basic questions.

1) Have we recently made some sacrificial choices in His behalf?

2) Are we spending much time in His presence?

Over the last few weeks we have been looking at how Jesus lived His life, and then seeing how we can live like He did. Today, I want us to see that we are able to do what Jesus would do. We are not living in the realm of theory or idealism, but we are talking about really living our lives as Jesus lived His.

In Luke 10 Christ sends out 72 disciples to represent Him among the cities of Judea. He called these disciples to go and make other people uncomfortable. We don't like to do that, do we? We ourselves are put off by false cults that may try to get our attention in an airport. Yet, that is precisely the kind of "uncomfortableness" Christ might be asking us to generate as we represent Him in this world.

Have you ever felt inadequate to be Christ's representative? I'm sure we all have. But in Luke chapter 10 we have five resources that God gives to those whom He sends out – resources that enable us to do everything that He commands and expects.

1. BECAUSE WE ARE COMMISSIONED

Luke 10:1

2. BECAUSE WE ARE PROTECTED

Luke 10:3

3. BECAUSE WE ARE INSTRUCTED

Luke 10:4-6

4. BECAUSE WE ARE EMPOWERED

Luke 10:9

Luke 10:19

5. BECAUSE WE ARE SECURE

Luke 10:18

Luke 10:20

Helpful Truths from Hebrews:
"The Need for Blood"

Introduction:

According to the Stanford Medical School Blood Center, "Blood is a living tissue composed of cellular elements and a watery fluid called plasma. "The cellular parts – red cells, white cells, and platelets, make up about 45% of the volume of whole blood. Plasma, which is 92% water, makes up the remaining 55%. Approximately 7% of a person's weight is blood. An average size man has about 12 pints of blood, and an average size woman has about 9 pints."

Keeping enough healthy blood in our systems is necessary for our life. But what is even more important to our lives is the shedding of blood. I am not talking about the ancient practice of "blood-letting", but of the importance of the shed blood of Jesus Christ. The Shedding of Blood is indispensable to our understanding of who we are and who we can become in Christ.

As we begin our new series, "Helpful Truths from Hebrews," we begin with one of the most important truths of all – Our Need for Blood – specifically, the blood of Jesus Christ. *Indeed, under the law almost everything is purified with blood, and without the shedding of blood there is no forgiveness of sins.* – **Hebrews 9:22 (ESV)**

1. THE SIGNIFICANCE OF BLOOD

1) In our Physical Lives

2) In our Spiritual Lives

Revelation 12:11

2. THE SACRIFICE OF BLOOD

Hebrews 12:2

Romans 3:10-18

1 John 4:10

3. THE SUFFICIENCY OF BLOOD

1) It Brings Removal

Hebrews 9:22

2) It Brings Return

Ephesians 2:13

3) It Brings Remembrance

Matthew 26:28

Helpful Truths from Hebrews: "The Need for Faith"

Introduction:

In a Peanuts comic strip, there was a conversation between Lucy and Charlie Brown. Lucy said "life is like a deck chair. Some place it so they can see where they are going; some place it so they can see where they have been; and some place it so they can see where they are at present." Charlie Brown's reply: "I can't even get mine unfolded."

Some of us are like Charlie Brown when it comes to our faith. We have trouble when it comes to seeing how God has worked in our lives and the life of our church and how He will work through us in the future. We've accepted Christ as our Savior but we have trouble getting out of the starting gate.

Hebrews 11:6 gives us a startling pronouncement about faith:

And without faith it is impossible to please him, for whoever would draw near to God must believe that he exists and that he rewards those who seek him. – **Hebrews 11:6 (ESV)**

This "faith" that Hebrews 11:6 describes is not the initial act of faith in Christ that saves us, it is describing the kind of faith that keeps us going in our Christian walk and that brings pleasure to God.

Now, if we are to please God there are two aspects of faith that must be demonstrated: We must believe that 1) He Exists; 2) He Rewards. Rather than going into a drawn out discussion of what this means, the writer to the Hebrews lists a number of examples for us of men/women who had this kind of faith that pleases God. Today I would like for us to focus on one of these examples to see how we might also please God.

The story of Abraham comes down to us from ancient times. He stands as the ideal which successive generations claimed. In him, men recognized the spirit which seemed to make life great. But how could a man be great who could be described in such words as those found in v. 8:

By faith Abraham obeyed when he was called to go out to a place that he was to receive as an inheritance. And he went out, not knowing where he was going. – **Hebrews 11:8 (ESV)**

Doesn't that run contrary to what we would say is "great"? *"He went out, not knowing where he was going."* What sort of leadership can we look for from one whom, when he starts out, does not know where he is going?

Well, Abraham wasn't really quite like that. His story is the story of a man who went out from his own surroundings into a country he had never seen — following an inward moving of faith, which as yet had no sufficient proof — he had no visible success — but at the end of his life we see he had so vast a success that all of history is awed by it.

Abraham, is of course, known for his great faith. Would you like to have a faith like Abraham's? Would you like to be a man/woman who lives for tomorrow? Would you like to be able to demonstrate a trust in God that keeps you moving forward toward the Promised Land? Well, we can have all of that, and more, if we follow the example set before us.

There are three areas of Abraham's life worthy of our consideration today — and by considering these three areas we will have three goals worthy of our attention and imitation:

1. THE IMPULSE OF FAITH

Genesis 12:1

2. THE EXPERIENCE OF FAITH

Hebrews 11:8

3. THE RESULT OF FAITH

Hebrews 11:10

Helpful Truths from Hebrews: "The Need for Holiness"

Introduction:

In Eugene Peterson's book, *A Long Obedience in the Same Direction*, he makes this powerful statement: "It is not difficult in our world to get a person interested in the message of the Gospel; it is terrifically difficult to sustain the interest. Millions of people in our culture make decisions for Christ, but there is a dreadful attrition rate. Many claim to have been born again, but the evidence for mature Christian discipleship is slim. In our kind of culture anything, even news about God, can be sold if it is packaged freshly; but when it loses its novelty, it goes on the garbage heap. There is a great market for religious experience in our world; there is little enthusiasm for the patient acquisition of virtue, little inclination to sign up for a long apprenticeship in what earlier generations of Christians called holiness."

I wish that I could disagree with Eugene Peterson, but he hits the nail right on the head. Many of us are prone to ignore the words of today's text:

Strive for peace with everyone, and for the holiness without which no one will see the Lord. – **Hebrews 12:14 (ESV)**

Essential to the Christian life is a constant pursuit of holiness. Being a Christian does not just involve making a decision for Christ – it is a life long journey that involves the discipline of living a life of holiness and bringing pleasure to God.
As we continue to look at Helpful Truths from Hebrews, we need to understand what holiness is, and how we can be holy people.

1. HOLINESS – A DEFINITION

1) Separation

1 Peter 2:9

2) Sinlessness/Purity

Habakkuk 1:13

Isaiah 6:5

2. HOLINESS – A RECEPTION

Romans 6:22

Ephesians 1:4

Ephesians 4:24

Romans 3:21-23

3. HOLINESS – A DEMONSTRATION

Hebrews 12:14

1 Peter 1:15-16

1 Thessalonians 4:7

Helpful Truths from Hebrews: "The Need for Discipline"

Introduction:

What is your first thought when you hear the word "discipline"? When I was a child, if you mentioned the word "discipline," I would have instantly pictured my father with a belt in one hand and me in the other one. As a parent I think more of the outcome of discipline with my children than I do the means by which it is carried out. As a Christian I think of the "spiritual disciplines" of Bible study, prayer, fasting, church attendance, and other things along those lines.

But when I read what the Bible has to say about discipline, I become a little uncomfortable. The Bible refers to us as the ones being disciplined and as God being the One doing the disciplining. I'd like to share with you a few select verses before we get to our text in Hebrews:

"Behold, blessed is the one whom God reproves; therefore despise not the discipline of the Almighty." – **Job 5:17 (ESV)**

For I am with you to save you, declares the LORD; I will make a full end of all the nations among whom I scattered you, but of you I will not make a full end. I will discipline you in just measure, and I will by no means leave you unpunished. – **Jeremiah 30:11 (ESV)**

Those whom I love, I reprove and discipline, so be zealous and repent. – **Revelation 3:19 (ESV)**

The Bible clearly teaches us that just as we have to discipline our children, so, too, God has to discipline us. In fact, discipline is necessary if we are to become the people God wants us to be.

In your struggle against sin you have not yet resisted to the point of shedding your blood. And have you forgotten the exhortation that addresses you as sons? "My son, do not regard lightly the discipline of the Lord, nor be weary when reproved by him. For the Lord disciplines the one he loves, and chastises every son whom he receives." It is for discipline that you have to endure. God is treating you as sons. For what son is there whom his father does not discipline? If you are left without discipline, in which all have participated, then you are illegitimate children and not sons. Besides this, we have had earthly fathers who disciplined us and we respected them. Shall we not much more be subject to the Father of spirits and live? For they disciplined us for a short time as it seemed best to them, but he disciplines us for our good, that we may share his holiness. For the moment all discipline seems painful rather than pleasant, but later it yields the peaceful fruit of righteousness to those who have been trained by it. – **Hebrews 12:4-11 (ESV)**

There are three aspects to God's Discipline that we need to understand today.

1. THE DEFINITION OF GOD'S DISCIPLINE

Matthew 11:29

2. THE DIMENSIONS OF GOD'S DISCIPLINE

1) Punishment

2 Samuel 12:10

1 Corinthians 11:32

2) Prevention

2 Corinthians 12:7

3) Education

Psalm 94:12

Proverbs 12:1

3. THE DIVIDENDS OF GOD'S DISCIPLINE

1) God's discipline provides proof that we are His children.

Hebrews 12:6

2) God's discipline promotes holiness in our lives.

Hebrews 12:10-11

3) God's discipline provides peace in our hearts.

Modern Family: "A Family with Purpose"

Introduction:

A sixth grade teacher in California, for a creative writing assignment, asked the children to complete the statement, "I wish...." Of course, she thought the kids would say things like, "I wish I had a bicycle," or "I wish I had a XBox," or "I wish I could go to Hawaii." Much to her surprise, 20 of the 30 in her class wished for things in their family to be better.

Let me read a few: One kid said, "I wish my parents wouldn't fight, and I wish my father would come back." Another one said, "I wish my mother didn't have a boyfriend." "I wish I could get straight A's so that my father would love me." "I wish I had one mom and one dad so the kids wouldn't make fun of me. I have three moms and three dads, and they botch up my life."

Today we are launching a new series called "Modern Family." But unlike the TV Show, we are going to focus on what it means to be a modern family that is grounded on biblical principles and the love of God. What I want to do is help families in some very practical areas of life. Today I want to focus on building a strong family which will help us answer the question, "What's a family for? What is our purpose?"

The idea for today's message is taken from a survey by two professors, from the University of Alabama and the University of Tennessee. In 50 newspapers in 25 different states, they put a short ad into the paper which basically said this: "If you live in a strong family, please contact us. We know a lot about what makes families fail. We need to know more about what makes them succeed."

From that little survey, they received over 3,000 responses from strong families. And, interestingly, as they compiled the responses, they discovered that everyone was saying basically the same thing. They compiled five key ingredients for a strong family, and the amazing thing is, they line up exactly with what the Bible has to say on the subject.

FIVE KEYS FOR STRONG FAMILIES

1. COMMITMENT

Ephesians 5:21

Ephesians 5:22

Ephesians 5:25

Proverbs 17:6

2. TIME TOGETHER

Psalm 68:6a

3. APPRECIATION

Proverbs 18:22

Proverbs 21:19

4. COMMUNICATION

5. SPIRITUAL HEALTH

Genesis 18:19

Joshua 24:14-15

Joshua 24:31

Modern Family: "A Family in Peace"

Introduction:

[14]A young rabbi found a serious problem in his new congregation. During the Friday service, half the congregation stood for the prayers and half remained seated, and each side shouted at the other, insisting that theirs was the true tradition. Nothing the rabbi said or did helped solve the impasse.

Finally, in desperation, the young rabbi sought out the synagogue's 99-year-old founder. He met the old rabbi in the nursing home and poured out his troubles. "So tell me," he pleaded, "was it the tradition for the congregation to stand during the prayers?" "No," answered the old rabbi. "Ah," responded the younger man, "then it was the tradition to sit during the prayers." "No," answered the old rabbi.

"Well," the young rabbi responded, "what we have is complete chaos! Half the people stand and shout and the other half sit and scream." "Ah," said the old rabbi, "that was the tradition."

The tradition in this young rabbi's synagogue is, unfortunately, the tradition in many of our homes. We've fought with each other for so long that it seems to be the norm. Today we're continuing our series designed to help you strengthen your family, and we want to discover how to restore harmony in your home.

If a house is divided against itself, that house will not be able to stand. – **Mark 3:25 (ESV)**

I think we all know the truth of that statement – in fact, some of us are living out that truth statement today. So let's see what we can do to change this for those of you that are presently going through a period of conflict, and also help those who aren't presently in conflict so that you'll be equipped to handle it when it comes. Today we want to look at three areas:

---

[14] P. J. ALINDOGAN, The Potter's Jar BLOG, "COMMUNICATE AND RELATE" (9-4-11)

---

1. THE REASON FOR CONFLICT

James 4:1-2a

2. THE REACTIONS TO CONFLICT

1) MY WAY

2) NO WAY

3) YOUR WAY

4) HALF WAY

5) OUR WAY

3. THE RESOLUTION TO CONFLICT

1) BECOME A CHRISTIAN

Ephesians 2:16

2) TALK TO GOD ABOUT IT

James 4:2b

3) ANALYZE THE PROBLEM

Matthew 7:3-4

4) SCHEDULE A PEACE CONFERENCE

Matthew 5:23-24

5) SWITCH YOUR FOCUS

Philippians 2:4-5

6) ASK FOR ADVICE

Proverbs 12:15

Modern Family: "A Family in Process"

Introduction:

James Dobson has a book entitled *Parenting Isn't for Cowards.* It is tough being a parent – just about the time you get experienced at it your kids go out the door.

There are many confusing voices today offering many different opinions about how to be a good parent. One guy had five theories and no kids and later he had five kids and no theories.

Where do you go for help? Who do you look to when you need help and advice on parenting? Who is our model? There is only one parent who has ever been perfect in history – that's our Heavenly Father.

You therefore must be perfect, as your heavenly Father is perfect. – **Matthew 5:48 (ESV)**

God is the model parent and the simple secret to effective parenting is to treat your kids the way God treats you. With that in mind, today I want us to look at what God is like and what He's about and then draw from that some applications for the parenting task. If I'm going to be like my Heavenly Father I must understand my children.

As a father shows compassion to his children, so the LORD shows compassion to those who fear him. For he knows our frame; he remembers that we are dust. – **Psalm 103:13-14 (ESV)**

God knows what makes us tick; He understands us. If I'm going to be a good parent like God, I need to understand my kids.

YOUR KIDS NEED...

1. UNDERSTANDING

Proverbs 24:3

Proverbs 22:6

2. ACCEPTANCE

> Romans 15:7

3. DISCIPLINE

> Hebrews 12:6

> Proverbs 13:24

> Proverbs 19:18

> **Do it Calmly**

> Proverbs 29:11

> **Do it Quickly**

> **Do it Sparingly**

> Colossians 3:21

4. LOVE

> **Affection**

> Psalm 145:9

> **Affirmation**

> Psalm 145:14

> **Attention**

> Psalm 145:18

5. CONSISTENCY

> Psalm 145:17

Modern Family: "A Family in Recovery"

Introduction:

We've been looking at the Modern Family over the last few weeks – not the one on TV, but the ones that live in our houses – and so far we've learned about *A Family with Purpose, A Family in Peace*, and *A Family in Process* – today we're going to tackle one of the most difficult issues that a family sometimes has to face. This message today is for those of you that have raised your kids in the Christian faith but for whatever reason, they have chosen to walk away.

Why do kids of godly parents go astray? I don't know the answer to that question; I think there are probably many. All through the Bible many godly parents had kids that went hay-wire. Adam, Noah, Samuel, Eli, Daniel, David... all had kids that went astray. Even today many godly parents have kids that go the wrong way and I'm not here to tell you why that happens, because I don't know why.

Today I want us to look at a passage of scripture that shows not *why* they go wrong but *what to do* when your kids rebel. There are three stages in a typical child's rebellion and we see all three of them in the story of the prodigal son.

And he said, "There was a man who had two sons. And the younger of them said to his father, 'Father, give me the share of property that is coming to me.' And he divided his property between them." – **Luke 15:11-12 (ESV)**

1. STAGE ONE: REBELLION

Luke 15:13

What Do You Do?

1) You Let Them Go

2) You Let Them Make Their Own Mistakes

3) You Let Them Reap the Consequences

Luke 15:14-16

2. STAGE TWO: RE-EVALUATION and REGRET

Luke 15:17-19

What Do You Do?

1) Pray

2) Commit Them to God

3) Wait Patiently

3. STAGE THREE: RETURN

Luke 15:20

What Do You Do?

1) Love Them Faithfully

2) Accept Them Unconditionally

...his father saw him and felt compassion, and ran and embraced him and kissed him.

Luke 15:21

3) Forgive Them Completely

Luke 15:22-24

Light it Up!: "Receive It"

Introduction:

[15]A website called the "Experience Project" describes itself as the place to share "life experiences from people like you." (As of March 2015 the site has had over 36 million experiences shared.) Visitors to the site are asked to share their thoughts about life experiences by answering questions like "What does loneliness feel like?" or "Who do you want to spend time with?" or "What is your favorite pastime?"

In one post, readers were asked to respond to the following statement: *"I prefer darkness over light."* A young woman going by the screen name "Beyond Repair" offered a particularly honest—and insightful—response:

"I prefer darkness over light. The darkness allows me to hide who I am and what I truly feel. In the light all things have a chance to be revealed .... Darkness makes it easier to hide. In the dark you cannot see what is coming next .... The darkness is a place where you can lose yourself. Lost in the dark is a great place to be because then you are free from what you were and can be what you want. The darkness is bliss."

I don't know how many people would be as frank as this girl was, but I do know that a lot of people feel the same way. And then there are others who are living in a dark place, yet they yearn for the light.

The Bible uses the terms *light* and *darkness* to describe the difference between living in a world without Christ and living in a world with Christ. In this series, "Light it Up" we want to focus on obtaining the light, living in the light, and sharing the light. Today we want to focus on how to come into the light of Jesus Christ.

---

[15] www.experienceproject.com

One of Jesus' reasons coming to this earth in human flesh was to show us how we might be transformed and subsequently, how we might transform our world.

And Jesus cried out and said, "Whoever believes in me, believes not in me but in him who sent me. And whoever sees me sees him who sent me. I have come into the world as light, so that whoever believes in me may not remain in darkness." – **John 12:44-46 (ESV)**

"I have come into the world as a light", Jesus said. What kind of light is He talking about? What does this light do?

1. JESUS OFFERS US THE LIGHT OF ACCESS

1) The access is to God the Father.

John 12:44-45

Matthew 10:40

2) This access to the Father only comes through the light – Jesus Christ.

John 14:6

2. JESUS OFFERS US THE LIGHT OF KNOWLEDGE

1) Knowledge of God.

2 Corinthians 4:6

2) Knowledge of Ourselves.

John 3:19-21

3) Knowledge of who we can become.

John 12:46

John 12:36a

3. JESUS OFFERS US THE LIGHT OF SALVATION

1) Jesus doesn't want you to remain outside of the light.

2) Jesus provides a way for you to be saved.

John 3:18

1 John 5:12

John 3:5

3) There is no reason for any of us to remain in darkness.

Light it Up!: "Live It"

Introduction:

[16]As an undergraduate, theologian/author D.A. Carson co-led an evangelistic Bible study. He confessed that whenever he felt out of his depths, he would take skeptics and doubters to a bold witness on campus named Dave. On one such occasion, a young man who was brought to Dave said, "I came from a family that doesn't believe in a literal resurrection and all that stuff. That's a bit much for us. But we're a fine family—a good, church-going family. We love each other, care for each other, and we do good in the community. We're a stable family. So what have you got that we don't have?"

Dave looked at the young man and said, "Watch me. Move in with me. I have an extra bed. Just follow me around. You see how I behave, what's important to me, what I do with my time, the way I talk. You watch me, and at the end of three months you tell me there's no difference."

The young man didn't take Dave up on that offer, but he did keep coming back to watch how Dave lived his Christian life. Eventually the young man came to Christ and went on to become a medical missionary. Carson concluded what he learned from Dave's challenge:

A Christian is saying in effect: "I'm one poor beggar telling another poor beggar where there's bread. I drank deeply from the wellsprings of grace. God knows I need more of it. If you watch me you'll see some glimmerings of the Savior, and ultimately you'll want to fasten on him. Watch me."

What a wonderful example that is of living out your faith, and shining the light of Christ in a world of darkness. As someone has said, "You are the only Jesus some people see." In other words, as

---

[16] BASED ON D.A. CARSON'S SERMON TITLED "BIBLICAL AUTHORITY: THE EXCLUSIVE AUTHORITY OF SCRIPTURE FOR FAITH AND PRACTICE" (2008)

His representative, you need to make sure you are a good example of the life He wants you to live.

In this series, "Light it Up" we want to learn how to obtain the light, be an example of the light, and share the light. The question before us today is: How can we shine the light in a world of darkness? We're going to answer that by looking at 2 Corinthians 4.

1. REMAIN POSITIVE IN A NEGATIVE WORLD

2 Corinthians 4:1

2. DEMONSTRATE INTEGRITY IN A DECEPTIVE WORLD

John 3:19-20

2 Corinthians 4:2

3. PRACTICE SERVANTHOOD IN A SELFISH WORLD

2 Corinthians 4:5

Matthew 20:25-28

4. MAINTAIN AUTHENTICITY IN A PHONY WORLD

1 John 2:15-17

2 Corinthians 4:7

Light it Up!: "Share It"

Introduction:

[17]A person is lying on a surgical table. It's the moment of crisis. Doctors and nurses are working frantically to save a life. But it's clear they are losing their patient. Next to the operating table, the EKG shows the patient's heartbeat. It's erratic. It's fading. It is gone.

A loud, high-decibel drone sounds, and a flat line appears on the monitor. The heart has stopped. Instead of giving up, the medical team increases its activity. The head doctor calls for a crash cart. Paddles are amped up with electrical current and pressed against the patient's chest. The doctor calls, "Clear!" and shocks the patient's heart. All eyes again turn toward the monitor with anticipation, fear, and hope.

Nothing. Still, the doctor is not ready to give up. "Clear!" Again, current is sent through the heart. All eyes are turn toward the monitor. Then another, and another. The heart is beating once again. Blood is flowing. A life has been saved.

Those of us who are Christians are in the life-saving business too. We are called by Christ to share our faith and as a result, see more and more people give their lives over to Jesus so that they might spend eternity with Him.

In Matthew 28:18-20 and in Acts 1:8 we find what is known as "The Great Commission." In this commission instructions are given to Jesus to all of His disciples – both then and now. Let's listen to His words:

And Jesus came and said to them, "All authority in heaven and on earth has been given to me. Go therefore and make disciples of all nations, baptizing them in the name of the Father and of the Son and

---

[17] KEVIN G. HARNEY, *Organic Outreach for Churches* (ZONDERVAN, 2011), PP. 19-20

of the Holy Spirit, teaching them to observe all that I have commanded you. And behold, I am with you always, to the end of the age." – **Matthew 28:18-20 (ESV)**

"But you will receive power when the Holy Spirit has come upon you, and you will be my witnesses in Jerusalem and in all Judea and Samaria, and to the end of the earth." – **Acts 1:8 (ESV)**

From these Words of Christ we learn that every believer in Christ not only has a potential to share their faith, but has a field for witness which we might or might not be aware of. Today, as we talk about sharing the light of Christ, there are three facts we need to etch into our hearts and minds.

1. YOU WILL NEVER MEET ANYONE WHO DOES NOT NEED WHAT GOD HAS TO OFFER IN JESUS CHRIST

2. YOU WILL NEVER MEET ANYONE WHO IS NOT THE OBJECT OF GOD'S LOVE AND CONCERN

3. YOU HAVE A PERSONAL REPONSIBILITY TO REACH OUT TO OTHERS IN THE NAME OF JESUS CHRIST

It's All About Jesus: "Jesus: Our Example"

Introduction:

[18]At the age of 23, Second Lieutenant Karl Marlantes was in charge of 40 marines during an intense battle in the Vietnam War. Marlantes had moved his men into the jungle as they waited for U.S. jets to bomb a hill that North Vietnamese soldiers had overtaken. Unfortunately, the jets came and dropped their bombs on the wrong hill. So when Marlantes led his men out of the jungle, they were instantly under fire from untouched machine-gun positions. Marlantes knew it would only take a few minutes before the enemy rockets and mortars found his troops. The entire mission ground to a halt as the U.S. soldiers ducked behind downed trees and huddled in shell holes.

Marlantes knew what he had to do next. He writes:

"If I didn't get up and lead, we'd get wiped out .... I did a lot of things that day ... but the one I'm most proud of is that I simply stood up, in the middle of that flying metal, and started up the hill .... I simply ran forward up the steep hill, zigzagging for the bunker, all by myself, hoping [my own soldiers] wouldn't hit me in the back. It's hard to zigzag while running uphill loaded down with ammunition and grenades."

But then in the midst of his solo charge up the hill to take out the enemy, Marlantes suddenly saw some movement in his peripheral vision:

"It was a marine! He was about 15 meters below me, zigzagging, falling, up and running again. Immediately behind him a long ragged line of Marines came moving and weaving up the hill behind me. Behind the line were spots of crumpled bodies, lying where they'd been hit. They'd all come with me .... Everyone was intermingled,

---

[18]KARL MARLANTES, "THE TRUTH ABOUT BEING A HERO," *The Wall Street Journal* (8-20-11)

weaving, rushing and covering, taking on each hole and bunker one at a time in groups .... WE, the group, just rushed forward all at once. WE couldn't be stopped. Just individuals among us were stopped ... but WE couldn't be .... I was we, no longer me."

As Christians we are called to follow Jesus in every way, even when that way might not be easy. That is what being a disciple of Christ is all about.

For to this you have been called, because Christ also suffered for you, leaving you an example, so that you might follow in his steps. – **1 Peter 2:21 (ESV)**

Let's look at a few examples Jesus set for us that He wants us to follow:

1. FOLLOW JESUS IN LOVING

John 13:34

John 13:35

2. FOLLOW JESUS IN WELCOMING

Romans 15:7

Matthew 25:35-40

3. FOLLOW JESUS IN FORGIVING

Colossians 3:12-13

It's All About Jesus: "Jesus: Our Power"

Introduction:

[19]Tim Keller tells the following story about the power of Christ's resurrection:

A minister was in Italy, and there he saw the grave of a man who had died centuries before who was an unbeliever and completely against Christianity, but a little afraid of it too. So the man had a huge stone slab put over his grave so he would not have to be raised from the dead in case there is a resurrection from the dead. He had insignias put all over the slab saying, "I do not want to be raised from the dead. I don't believe in it." Evidently, when he was buried, an acorn must have fallen into the grave. So a hundred years later the acorn had grown up through the grave and split that slab. It was now a tall towering oak tree. The minister looked at it and asked, "If an acorn, which has power of biological life in it, can split a slab of that magnitude, what can the acorn of God's resurrection power do in a person's life?"

Keller comments:

The minute you decide to receive Jesus as Savior and Lord, the power of the Holy Spirit comes into your life. It's the power of the resurrection—the same thing that raised Jesus from the dead .... Think of the things you see as immovable slabs in your life—your bitterness, your insecurity, your fears, your self-doubts. Those things can be split and rolled off. The more you know him, the more you grow into the power of the resurrection.

We are going to start with the power of Jesus' resurrection today and see that, while extremely important, it is one of many powers that Jesus displays.

---

[19]NANCY GUTHRIE, EDITOR, *Jesus, Keep Me Near the Cross* (CROSSWAY, 2009), P. 136

---

1. THE POWER OF HIS RESURRECTION

Philippians 3:10

John 5:28-29

2. THE POWER OF HIS GRACE

2 Corinthians 12:9

3. THE POWER OF HIS SPIRIT

Ephesians 3:16-19

4. THE POWER OF HIS PRESERVATION

1 Peter 1:3-5

5. THE POWER OF HIS LOVE

1 John 3:16-19

It's All About Jesus: "Jesus: Our Ransom"

Introduction:

[20]On a cold winter day Gabriel Estrada, a high school senior in Twin Lakes, Wisconsin, did the unthinkable. When his 17-year-old girlfriend secretly gave birth to a baby boy on January 15, 2002, she dressed it and asked him to deliver it to a church. Instead, Gabriel wrapped the baby in a canvas bag and left him in a portable toilet in a nearby park to die. But against incredible odds the baby was saved.

According to police there was virtually no chance the infant would survive. Temperatures were well below freezing. Lack of snow meant the nearby sledding hill would not be frequented by kids. And the sanitation company's scheduled pick-up at the port-a-potty was days away.

Village of Twin Lakes police credit a father and son for saving the child's life. About 4 o'clock in the afternoon on January 16th a father (wishing to remain anonymous) and his young son stopped at the abandoned West Side Park in need of a bathroom. Hearing a whimpering sound coming from the port-a-potty, they knew something was wrong. They called 911 to report what they had discovered.

When Officer Randy Prudik responded to the call, he pulled the canvas bag from the outdoor toilet and raced to nearby Burlington Memorial Hospital where the baby received emergency treatment.

"There's no way he would have survived that," Prudik said. "That little guy had somebody watching over him."

As a testament to the boy's survival, the nurses at the hospital dubbed him William Grant: William for the will to live and Grant for not taking life for granted.

---

[20]MILWAUKEE JOURNAL SENTINEL (1-7-02)

On a grander scale, another Father and Son rescue team intervened on behalf of doomed humanity:

For there is one God, and there is one mediator between God and men, the man Christ Jesus, who gave himself as a ransom for all, which is the testimony given at the proper time. **- 1 Timothy 2:5-6 (ESV)**

To free us from our life of sin and damnation a ransom had to be paid, and the only payment that would suffice was the life of Jesus Christ, the Son of God.

1. A RANSOM GIVEN AS A GIFT OF LOVE

John 3:16

2. A RANSOM GIVEN AS PAYMENT FOR OUR SIN

Galatians 1:3-4

Titus 2:14

3. A RANSOM GIVEN AS OUR SUBSTITUTE

2 Corinthians 5:21

Matthew 20:28

John 6:51

4. A RANSOM GIVEN AS A REMEMBRANCE

Luke 22:19-20

It's All About Jesus:
"Jesus: Our Coming One"

Introduction:

[21]In the 2007 film THE BUCKET LIST, two terminally ill men—played by Jack Nicholson and Morgan Freeman—take a road trip to do the things they always said they would do before they "kicked the bucket." In anticipation of the film's release, Nicholson was interviewed for an article in Parade magazine. While reflecting on his personal life, Nicholson said:

I used to live so freely. The mantra for my generation was "Be your own man!" I always said, "Hey, you can have whatever rules you want—I'm going to have mine. I'll accept the guilt. I'll pay the check. I'll do the time." I chose my own way. That was my philosophical position well into my 50s. As I've gotten older, I've had to adjust.

But reality has a way of getting the attention of even a Jack Nicholson. Later in the interview, Nicholson adds:

We all want to go on forever, don't we? We fear the unknown. Everybody goes to that wall, yet nobody knows what's on the other side. That's why we fear death.

While a Christian might have some trepidation about facing the unknown, we do not need to share Jack Nicholson's fear of death. Jesus has promised us a heavenly home that we will share with Him for all of eternity.

"And if I go and prepare a place for you, I will come again and will take you to myself, that where I am you may be also." – **John 14:3 (ESV)**

---

[21] DOTSON RADER, "I WANT TO GO ON FOREVER," *Parade* MAGAZINE (12-9-07), PP. 6-8

Let's break this verse down and take a little time to examine every wonderful part of Jesus' promise.

1. THE PERSON – *"I"*

>Colossians 2:9

>Hebrews 1:3a

2. THE PROMISE – *"I will come again."*

>2 Peter 3:3-4

>1 Thessalonians 4:15-18

3. THE PEOPLE – *"And will take you to myself."*

>(refer to 1 Thessalonians 4:15-18 above)

4. THE PLACE – *"That where I am."*

>Colossians 3:1

>Ephesians 1:20

>Acts 7:55-56

5. THE PURPOSE – *"You may be also."*

>John 14:1-3

IMPORTANT NOTE:

If you would like to receive brand new sermons each and every month, please consider our service at:

www.SermonSubscription.com

We offer several different levels of membership, from detailed Sermon Starters, as seen in this book, to full manuscript messages, complete with PowerPoint and congregational handouts.

Many other dynamic resources are offered at:

www.PastorsHelper.com

Made in the USA
Middletown, DE
05 February 2023

24104682R00086